HERMIT OF GO CLIFFS

HERMIT OF GO CLIFFS

TIMELESS INSTRUCTIONS

from a TIBETAN MYSTIC

Translated and Introduced by

Cyrus Stearns

WISDOM PUBLICATIONS • BOSTON

Wisdom Publications
199 Elm Street
Somerville MA 02144

Library of Congress Cataloging-in-Publication Data

Ko-brag-pa Bsod-nams-rgyal-mtshan, 1170–1249.
[Ko-brag-pa'i mgur 'bum. English and Tibetan]
Hermit of Go Cliffs : timeless instructions from a Tibetan mystic / translated and introduced by Cyrus Stearns.
p. cm.
Includes bibliographical references and index.
ISBN 0-86171-164-5 (alk. paper)
1. Ko-brag-pa Bsod-nams-rgyal-mtshan, 1170–1249.
2. Spiritual life—Buddhism—Early works to 1800.
3. Lamas—China—Tibet—Biography—Early works to 1800.
4. Buddhist meditations—Early works to 1800.
I. Stearns, Cyrus, 1949– II. Title.

BQ968.027 A3 2000
294.3'923'092—dc21
[B] 99-088201

ISBN 0-86171-164-5

05 04 03 02 01
6 5 4 3 2

Design: Gopa and MacBear
Cover Photo: Samding Monastery, the home of the Samding Dorje Phagmo, the only incarnation line of female teachers in Tibet. Photo by Andy Quintman.

Wisdom Publications' books are printed on acid-free paper and meet the guidelines for the permanence and durability of the Production Guidelines for Book Longevity of the Council on Library Resources.

Printed in the United States of America

CONTENTS

ILLUSTRATIONS

PUBLISHER'S ACKNOWLEDGMENT

THE PUBLISHER gratefully acknowledges the generous help of the Hershey Family Foundation in sponsoring the publication of this book.

PREFACE & ACKNOWLEDGMENTS

THE SELECTIVE RECORDS of history provide only glimpses of scenes from the past. I have always felt drawn to figures and stories barely visible in the historical landscape. From the late Dezhung Rinpoche, who was a matchless example of the nonsectarian *(ris med)* approach to realization, I first heard about the lives and teachings of many great Tibetan masters, ancient and modern. After receiving the teachings of the Path with the Result *(Lam 'bras)* from Chogye Trichen Rinpoche in 1982, I began reading the historical accounts of this tradition. One of the obscure early Tibetan masters of the Path with the Result was known as Godrakpa *(Ko brag pa),* or "Man of Go Cliffs." I was intrigued by descriptions of him as someone who combined the practices of the Path with the Result and those of the Six-Branch Yoga of the Kālacakra, but I was frustrated to find only a few sentences about him in the historical records. Some years later I received the teachings of the Six-Branch Yoga from Chogye Rinpoche and found mention of Godrakpa in the histories of this tradition. Moreover, I learned that Godrakpa had been one of the main teachers of the important Drukpa Kagyu master Yangönpa. But who was this elusive "Hermit of Go Cliffs," whose story and teachings seemed to have vanished over the centuries?

The extremely influential nonsectarian movement of nineteenth century Tibet is familiar to many students of Tibetan religious history. Names that emerged at this time, such as Jamyang Khyentse Wangpo, Jamgön Kongdrul, and Jamgön Mipham, are among the most renowned in Tibet. These masters built their movement on a foundation of examples set by earlier, broad-minded scholars and meditators who appreciated the diversity of the different paths to enlightenment followed in Tibet. Famous in his day, but almost unknown now, Godrakpa, the Hermit of Go Cliffs, was a remote forebear of this nonsectarian movement.

Before returning to the United States in 1991 after living for some years in

Kathmandu, I asked Franz-Karl Ehrhard, then director of the Nepal-German Manuscript Preservation Project, to be on the lookout for Godrakpa's rare *Collected Songs (Mgur 'bum),* which was known to have been printed in the sixteenth century at the ancient hermitage of Tragar Daso. Later, during a visit to Kathmandu in 1993, I was delighted to hear that an incomplete copy of the *Collected Songs* had been photographed by the Project, and with Franz-Karl's assistance I obtained a copy. Over the next few years, I often found inspiration in Godrakpa's moving verse and began to translate the incomplete collection for my own enjoyment. During this period I also received from Leonard van der Kuijp a small manuscript biography of Godrakpa that he had located in Beijing. At this point, I gradually began to piece together a book around the translation of Godrakpa's songs.

In the fall of 1998 I sent the book manuscript to E. Gene Smith at Wisdom Publications. Gene then told me that he also had an incomplete copy of the same edition of Godrakpa's *Collected Songs,* which he graciously retrieved from storage in France and sent to me. Since the two incomplete Tibetan texts are missing different pages, it is now possible to form a complete copy, which is here published for the first time in almost five hundred years. The Tibetan text reproduced in this volume is an almost exact duplication of the original Tragar Daso print. Texts from this printery are famous for their beautiful woodcut portraits of teachers and deities, but notorious for their horrific orthography. No attempt has been made here to "correct" the many unusual spellings in the original. The frequency of archaic terms and the prevalence of local idioms and spellings, some which still remain unclear, convinced me that "corrections" would simply create a new text that had never existed to begin with. A number of the more significant obscure terms and idioms are indicated in the notes. Often there are mere phonetic renderings of words, such as the homophones *rlungs, phyags, grub, zug, kyo, ig, chug,* and *bye,* instead of the correct *klung, chags, brub, gzugs, skyo, dbyig, phyug,* and *je,* and so forth. There is also some confusion of Tibetan letters with similar forms, such as *s, l,* and *m.* Since it is not practical to indicate all of these irregularities, and since many will be understood by readers of Tibetan, only the most cryptic have been singled out for mention in the notes. In most cases, corrupt spellings of personal and geographical names have been standardized in the translation, as have Sanskrit words.

Notes to the introduction have been placed immediately after the introduction. But in order not to distract the reader of the songs, note numbers have not been inserted into the translation. Notes to the translation are found immediately after the verses, listed by song number. Within the translation, small type has been used for everything added by the editor of the Tibetan text, and larger type has been used for Godrakpa's own words of introduction and conclusion, and for the songs themselves.

Without access to the rare original texts made available by E. Gene Smith, Franz-Karl Ehrhard, and Leonard van der Kuijp, this book could never have been written. I am grateful for their generous assistance. I also thank Tulku Sangak Rinpoche for kindly spending two summer afternoons in Seattle discussing difficult points in the Tibetan text. His explanation of archaic and regional terms was invaluable. Richard, Susan, and Melong Baldwin provided a wonderful environment in their garden for these discussions. I am also indebted to Andy Quintman, whose beautiful photographs greatly enhance the presentation of Godrakpa's songs. The skillful editorial pen of Victoria Scott made great improvements throughout the work. Hubert Decleer and Nazneen Zafar read an earlier version of the book, and their astute suggestions and words of encouragement helped me bring the work to completion. Jeff Schoening also kindly read through the text and made very helpful comments. I also thank Kurtis Schaeffer for first urging me to contact Wisdom Publications. Finally, I greatly enjoyed talking about the book with Sofia, Anna, and Tania.

INTRODUCTION

You meditate, but confusion isn't destroyed.
Don't you recognize the true nature right in front of you?
Lady Machik Zhama[1]

1. The Tradition

The story of Buddhism in Tibet is long, fascinating, and convoluted. What survives at the end of the twentieth century is a distillation of many different elements, each of which once formed a facet of the spiritual topography of that glacial land. When seeking to make sense of such a rich and complicated history, the great nineteenth-century master Jamgön Kongdrul (1813–99), who was instrumental in the revival of numerous Tibetan religious traditions, spoke of eight major systems of esoteric knowledge that had developed over the centuries.[2]

Most of these traditions appeared in Tibet after the second major influx of teachings from India and Nepal in the eleventh century and were originally centered in or near the southwestern border regions. For example, the tradition of the Path with the Result *(Lam 'bras)* slowly spread from the valley of Nyugu, where it was first taught by the charismatic Drokmi Lotsawa (993–1077?); the teachings of the equally eccentric Marpa Lotsawa (1000–1082) were first localized in his home region of Lhodrak; the transmission of the doctrine of Pacification *(Zhi byed)* was closely connected to the region of Tingri, where the intriguing Indian master Phadampa Sangye (d. 1105) made his residence; and the instructions of Severance *(Gcod)* were developed by the exceptional Lady Machik Labdrön (1055–1153) in the Bodong area, although she later lived in central Tibet.[3] Geographical exceptions were the teachings later known as Shangpa Kagyu, which were taught by Khyungpo Naljor (b. 990?) and his successors in the more northern Shang Valley, and the Gadam school, which took root in the northern region of Phenyul in Central Tibet. The extremely influential teachings of the Kālacakra were not connected with any specific area.

Prior to the thirteenth century, the rigid sectarian identities that would plague later Tibetan religious history had not yet fully crystallized, and the network of monasteries specifically connected to the major transmission lines was still in embryonic form. An eclectic approach to study and meditative realization was still commonplace. Individual teachers and practitioners were not identified according to allegiance to a specific sect, but more often simply by their primary site of teaching or practice, and were thought of as upholders of particular transmission lines of esoteric instruction.

By the middle of the thirteenth century, all the traditions that had come to Tibet in the eleventh century were firmly established and flourishing, as was the Nyingma tradition, as the lineages based on texts translated into Tibetan in the eighth and ninth centuries were now collectively called. From each tradition great teachers appeared who became reknowned throughout the country. But as the centuries passed and the major sects of the Nyingma, Sakya, Kagyu, and Geluk became increasingly dominant, several of the earlier vital traditions underwent radical transformation. Once strong and widespread, the Pacification teachings of Phadampa fell into relative obscurity outside the Tingri area. Lady Machik Labdrön's tradition of Severance gradually ceased to exist as an independent system, and her instruction lineages were largely absorbed into the Nyingma, Kagyu, and Geluk schools. The Shangpa Kagyu teachings were also practiced and taught by increasingly fewer independent followers, and were more often transmitted by representatives of the Kagyu, Jonang, and Sakya schools.

As a result of these developments, what is now known about the lives and teachings of great Tibetan masters of the tenth through the thirteenth centuries is often restricted to representatives of the lineages that later became dominant—namely, the Nyingma, Sakya, and Kagyu, as well as those of the Gadam, which were later adopted by the Geluk school. This is quite understandable. The original textual records of teachings that died out were naturally considered to be of less importance once they were no longer taught. When even the reading transmission of those texts died out, they could no longer be practiced. Likewise, the biographies of prominent masters in those traditions that fell into obscurity were often lost, again because they were not looked upon with the devotion and interest generated by the life stories of teachers who were regarded as the ancestors of the surviving schools.

Little but the names of numerous such important teachers have survived, even though some are briefly described in various sources as extremely influential. One master whose legacy nearly vanished during the last seven hundred years was known as Godrakpa, Sönam Gyaltsen (1170–1249), the "Man of Go Cliffs."[4]

Godrakpa was a teacher and yogin of extraordinary character and determination whose sole concern was the rigorous practice of meditation. He was particularly dedicated to the practice of the Path with the Result *(Lam 'bras)* in the tradition of the exceptional yoginī Lady Machik Zhama (1062–1149), concerning which he wrote a number of instruction manuals.[5] He was also instrumental in bringing a special lineage of the Six-Branch Yoga of Kālacakra to Tibet.[6] Nevertheless, even the authors of some of the most definitive histories of religion in Tibet remained uncertain about where to place him because of the widespread and eclectic nature of his practices and activities. At the end of the brief sketch of Godrakpa's life in *The Blue Annals*—the most comprehensive history of Buddhism in Tibet up through the fifteenth century—the author Gö Lotsawa Zhönu Bal (1392–1481) concludes with the following comment:

> I have written about this great individual separately because I do not know whether "he belongs within this Kagyu tradition."[7]

The Sakya master Mangtö Ludrup Gyantso (1523–96) could say only, "He practiced the Dakpo Kagyu, the Zhama tradition of the Path with the Result, and so forth."[8] Some two hundred years later, the Gelukpa historian Tukwan Chögyi Nyima (1737–1802), in his *Crystal Mirror of Philosophical Tenets*, was also uncertain about how to describe Godrakpa's views:

> There was no Dharma this master called Godrakpa Sönam Gyaltsen did not know. In particular, he was an expert in the removal of [yogic] impediments.[9] But I do not know just how he upheld the view and philosophical tenets because I have not seen any explanation. Nevertheless, since there were no learned and realized Tibetans during that time who did not touch his feet, his enlightened activities were very vast. He had many fine disciples and grand-disciples, but it seems that his specific philosophical tenets and specific Dharma transmission did not last long.[10]

Although specific transmissions of Godrakpa's own writings have not survived to the present day, his legacy certainly remained vital for much longer than Tukwan implies. For example, Jonang Kunga Trolchok (1507–66) received the transmission of an instruction manual on the practices of the Path with the Result composed by Godrakpa, as well as Godrakpa's most famous work, *A Sea of Visualizations of the Syllable HA for the Removal of Impediments (Gegs sel ha dmigs rgya mtsho).*[11] Moreover, some of Godrakpa's treatises on the Path with the Result were still being taught in the middle of the seventeenth century, some four hundred years after his death.[12] But why would the lineage of teachings from such a highly regarded master eventually fall into decline? Perhaps the main reason was that Godrakpa was intimately connected with traditions that were not upheld by the major schools as they developed after his lifetime.

Godrakpa is most remembered in the tradition of the Path with the Result. Other than the collection of his songs translated in the present work, the only texts he is known to have authored were concerned with the meditation practices of this tradition. Later historians all identify Godrakpa's teachings of the Path with the Result as one of the eighteen lineages of this tradition that developed in Tibet.[13] His instructions are usually described as representative of the "female transmission" *(mo rgyud)* of the Zhama lineage that came from Lady Machik Zhama—not the "male transmission" *(pho rgyud)* that came from her brother Lord Khumpuwa Chögyal (1069–1144) or the "combined transmission" *(bsres rgyud)* in which the instructions of both were mixed.[14]

But this Path with the Result transmission that Godrakpa upheld was a lineage that was never emphasized by a major, established sect. He was the most outstanding master of Lady Machik Zhama's Path with the Result, while his famous contemporary Sakya Paṇḍita (1182–1251) upheld and taught the Path with the Result of the Sakya tradition. This latter version became extremely widespread during Sakya Paṇḍita's lifetime and for many centuries thereafter, which explains the eventual eclipse of Godrakpa's teachings on the Path with the Result.

Godrakpa also practiced and taught a special direct transmission of the Six-Branch Yoga of the Kālacakra tantra, which was first taught to him in Tibet by the Indian master Vibhūticandra, who had received it in Kathmandu, Nepal, from the Indian adept Śavaripa, who is believed to have achieved immortality through his practice of tantric yoga. This set of instructions was also never embraced as the main practice of a major school, although it has continued to be transmitted to the present day in various lineages.[15]

In addition, Godrakpa was a practitioner of Phadampa's tradition of Pacification and of the meditation practices of the goddess Vajravārāhī that had been passed down from the Indian adept Lady Lakṣmīṅkarā. The non-sectarian nature of Godrakpa's approach is obvious in song 1. In short, he practiced and taught a wide variety of profound tantric systems, none of

Gyirong Valley

which were upheld as major traditions in any of the dominant schools that developed from the middle of the thirteenth century. As a result, this remarkable yogin's independent legacy can only be traced up through the middle of the seventeenth century.

More than anything else, Godrakpa emphasized the priority of meditation practice. He was radically dedicated to austere meditation in the isolated mountain ranges of southwest Tibet, a tradition he passed on to his disciples and expressed poetically in his songs. In many ways the style and the feeling conveyed by his songs bring to mind those of the great Kagyu master and poet Jetsun Milarepa (1028–1111), echoes of whose words are sometimes heard in Godrakpa's verse. Indeed, Godrakpa spent many years meditating in some of the same caves as Milarepa and was deeply influenced by his example. In fact, Lady Machik Zhama's lineage of the Path with the Result seems to have been transmitted primarily by early Kagyu teachers.

Nyö Chögyi Ziji (1164–1224), the only one of Godrakpa's three teachers of the Path with the Result who is well-known to history, was one of the main disciples of Jikden Gönpo (1143–1217), the founder of the Drigung Kagyu tradition. And Godrakpa's own most important disciple was the master Gyalwa Yangönpa (1213–58), an early prodigy of the Drukpa Kagyu tradition whose commitment to meditation is legendary. Yangönpa's writings demonstrate his devotion to Godrakpa and his own practice of the Path with the Result in the tradition of both Lady Machik Zhama and Godrakpa.

2. The Life

Only one short biography of Godrakpa is presently available, and Godrakpa himself provides some information about his life in his songs. Brief passages about him in the historical surveys of the Path with the Result and in a history of the Kālacakra teachings in Tibet focus on his role in the practice and transmission of those lineages. A glimpse into events and experiences of his life can be gained from these sources, and a more complete picture can be formed by splicing this information together with fragments found in other historical and doctrinal works. The following description of Godrakpa's life is based on the information and chronology found in the biography by Sherab Gön, which was written during or soon after Godrakpa's life, and is further enriched with material from the other sources.[16]

Godrakpa was born during the Tiger year of 1170 in the Tingri area near the border of Tibet and Nepal. His parents had been childless, but a great yoginī had given his father some food the year before the child's birth and had prophesied that a son would be born the next year whom they should raise carefully, because he would bring benefit to many living beings. In the first of the songs translated below, Godrakpa himself mentions that even as a small child he had no thought but to practice the Buddha's teachings. While still young he experienced a realization that the ephemeral appearances of daily life were not grounded in truth, and a deep faith and renunciation arose. In 1185, when he was fifteen years old, he began to practice the meditation of Vajrapāṇi, and the animate and inanimate world dawned as a divine maṇḍala.[17]

Godrakpa later stated that when he was eighteen years old he spent six months studying the Buddhist sūtras, recognized the harmful consequences inherent in a mundane lifestyle, and first learned about the vast enlightened activities of the bodhisattvas and the great qualities of buddhahood. These

The Tingri Plains

insights caused the birth of a sincere devotion and formed an armor to his meditation. After experiencing still further realization of the unreality of ordinary appearances, Godrakpa took the initial vows of a Buddhist layman from the master Semikpa. From this teacher he first received the transmission of many of the teachings he would practice for the rest of his life and would later pass on to the next generation. Of these, the most significant for Godrakpa's future were the profound instructions of the Path with the Result that had been passed down from Lady Machik Zhama.[18]

Then Godrakpa departed for some time to practice austerities and meditation in the mountains.[19]

When he later returned home for a visit, his family gave him much wealth and insisted that he assume the life of a householder. But the prospect revolted him, and he gave all the wealth away to beggars. At this point his father also renounced the householder's life to become a yogin and was so impressed with his son's dedication to meditation practice that he actually accompanied Godrakpa as his attendant. For some time after this, Godrakpa traveled around the land requesting teachings in different lineages from various masters, as he describes in song 1. During this period he performed several more mountain retreats, and the authentic realization of the Great Seal *(mahāmudrā)* arose in his mind. He also practiced the austerity of subsisting only on water for a long time.[20] Speaking about this time in his life, Godrakpa made the following statement:

> From the first I didn't chase after food and drink, nor experience delight in distracting spectacles. I practiced austerities and devoted myself to virtuous actions.... I received little assistance and was afraid of even being noticed by people. Other than thinking that I must practice and apply the meaning to my mindstream, I never imagined that I would have to teach others.[21]

Godrakpa decided to go to Nepal and India, but was prevented by his father from making the dangerous trip. He mentioned that during his travels he once saw the corpse of a leper woman and, feeling disgusted by it, ate some of her brains, which freed him from further conceptualizations about cleanliness and filth. Sometime during this period he also met the Newar master Ratnarakṣita and received from him the Cakrasaṃvara initiation. Once, when staying in a small guesthouse on the holy Mt. Shrī, Godrakpa saw others sleeping outside in the snow and rain. Out of compassion he built two large guesthouses for future visitors, using the fine houses of the area as models. Song 34 was sung on this occasion.[22]

While staying at the hermitage of Gyamring, Godrakpa became very ill and couldn't even walk. With the aim of recovery, he performed the propitiation of the wrathful deity Acala *(Mi g.yo ba),* and other practices. One day he was reading and pondering a text on the Four Truths according to the Pacification tradition when he realized that the illness was actually indispensable because it caused him to focus single-mindedly on virtuous actions. He became confident that he would gain realization if he remained ill for twelve years, and gained exceptional certainty that if he were healthy and lived in a fine house he would just be distracted. He stopped all the practices he had been doing to cure himself and went to sleep, but when he awoke he was cured. He couldn't believe it was true, walked back and forth, and realized he really was no longer ill. The experience strengthened his certainty in the Dharma. Godrakpa describes these events in his preface to song 8.

On another occasion he went to meditate in the Great Cave *(Phug mo che)* of Labchi north of Mt. Everest where Jetsun Milarepa had spent many years in meditation little more than a century before. Some followers of the Drigung Kagyu tradition showed up and told him to leave the cave. But there were also some meditators of the Tshal and Druk branches of the Kagyu school who claimed to have the same masters, lineage, and oral instructions and who refused to leave. As tension grew, Godrakpa remarked, "I came to practice Dharma. I didn't come to indulge in desire and anger and to accumulate sin." He offered them his dry wood and supplies and went off to stay in another place called Senge Drak. The other meditators were apparently chastised by his example because thereafter they referred to him as "the honorable and excellent master from Tingri" and brought him sanctified food from their tantric feasts.

During this retreat he decided that after coming to a mountain hermitage it wasn't right to just live in an ordinary fashion. This made him intensely energetic in meditation day and night. As a result, he encountered extreme obstacles, but the problems were resolved by allowing the natural expression of the experiences to occur, and his meditation was greatly enhanced. Godrakpa vividly describes these experiences in song 2, from which it is clear that he was meditating on the teachings of the Path with the Result during this retreat.[23]

For a long period during another retreat at Langkor, he experienced the sufferings of being born in hell.[24]

In another experience, while meditating on nearby Mt. Shrī, he was graced with a vision of a beautiful woman, actually the Indian adept Lady Lakṣmīṅkarā, who bestowed on him a brief teaching. This episode and Lakṣmīṅkarā's words are translated in song 20.[25]

Until this point Godrakpa had been living as a lay yogin, but when he was twenty-eight years old he requested the Dharma Lord Nyö Chögyi Ziji to grant him the vows of complete ordination as a Buddhist monk.[26]

Lord Nyö gave him the ordination name Sönam Gyaltsen, and, when a crash of thunder occurred at the same moment, the master exclaimed, "It is a fine, auspicious connection. You will become famous and have a great reputation." This teacher also bestowed on Godrakpa several teachings of the Drigung Kagyu tradition, of which he was an important master.

Following his ordination, Godrakpa took a single monk with him as an assistant and traveled west to Mt. Tise and Lake Mapham, where he meditated in seclusion for five years. He practiced continuous austerities, subsisting on the leaves of plants such as knotweed. As a result of his intense meditation, he actually beheld the face of the goddess Vajravārāhī and directly perceived the true state of the interior vajra body *(rdo rje lus kyi gnas lugs),* as well as many exterior pure lands. During this retreat he also had a dream of a woman who pledged to provide him with water wherever he stayed. She was actually the *nāga* spirit of the region, and Godrakpa stated that from then on water would appear wherever he resided, even in parched land.[27] Song 9 was sung during this time.

After a period of extended seclusion in the Tise region, Godrakpa returned to meditate in areas such as Semik and Mt. Shrī where he had done retreats before. During this time he experienced visions of the deities Cakrasaṃvara and Acala. At Nyanam, near the border with Nepal, he performed a retreat of 3.6 million repetitions of the mantra of Vajrayoginī and said that he experienced actually becoming Vajrayoginī herself. During his stay there his reputation spread, and when there began to be too much excitement among the people, he took a single assistant with him and fled. Soon thereafter he met the immortal Indian adept Saraha, one of the original masters of the Great Seal, who brought Godrakpa face to face with the nature of reality.[28] This dream vision is recorded in song 19.

He then stayed for a long time in the cave of Godrak ("Go Cliffs") in the Upper Nyang region, specifically in the upper valley of Zhalu.[29] While living in this cave he became known as the Dharma Lord Godrakpa. During this period he again met the master Nyö Chögyi Ziji, from whom he now received the instructions of the Path with the Result in the tradition of Lady Machik Zhama.[30] On his return journey to Godrak, he met the master Mönkhar Sherab Tsultrim, from whom he also requested Lady Zhama's Path with the Result.[31] After arriving back at Godrak, he taught the Path with the Result to approximately one hundred and twenty accomplished teachers.

Again Godrakpa traveled in nearby regions, visiting other great masters. During this trip he also received lavish honors from the ruler Shakya Ö at Chumik Ringmo, where he gave many Dharma teachings. On his return to Upper Nyang, he stayed at the cave of Rasa Chuphuk and taught many students for a long period.[32] According to later histories of the Path with the Result, Godrakpa lived in this cave for twenty-four years, during which time he devoted himself only to the meditations of the Path with the Result.[33] He is said to have gained boundless clairvoyance and magical abilities as a result and to have perceived all the key points of the subtle channels and vital winds. He experienced a visionary meeting with the immortal Lord of Yogins, Virūpa, who was the original human source of the Path with the Result, and then wrote numerous texts explaining the practices of that tradition.[34]

At some point, the number of people gathered around the cave where Godrakpa was living became too large and distracting. He took two men as assistants and fled in the dead of night, leaving behind the others in his circle, as well as all the valuables and presents that had been offered to him. He proceeded first to the monastery of Trophu, where he was welcomed by the famous translator Trophu Lotsawa (Jampay Bal, 1172–1236). But here also a great crowd gathered, and there were again huge offerings of food and valuables. Godrakpa offered the best things to Trophu Lotsawa and distributed the rest among the members of the Sangha. Then he fled in the night and traveled south, returning to his home region of Langkor in the Tingri border area.

In 1223, while Godrakpa was living in Tingri Langkor, a ten-year-old child prodigy known as Gyalwa Yangönpa came from the hermitage of Lhadong on nearby Mt. Shrī to meet him. All sources are unanimous in stating that Yangönpa became the most important of Godrakpa's many disciples and Dharma heirs. Yangönpa himself felt that Godrakpa had been his teacher through countless lifetimes. Between 1223 and 1234 Godrakpa bestowed on Yangönpa all of his teachings, initiations, and esoteric instructions, and participated in Yangönpa's final monastic ordination.[35]

In particular, Godrakpa taught his young student the meditation practices of the Path with the Result in the tradition of Lady Machik Zhama. There is abundant evidence that Yangönpa himself then practiced these instructions extensively.[36]

Sometime during this stay in Tingri Langkor, four ḍākinīs appeared to Godrakpa while he was in sealed retreat in the White Residence of Phadampa Sangye. Their brief song and Godrakpa's reply are translated in song 28. During this period Godrakpa is said to have saved the lives of thousands of poor people and beggars by distributing grain at a time of extreme shortage. He was also credited with turning back the threat of a Mongol invasion. At least one independent historical text records Godrakpa's request for twenty-three teachers to perform a rite for averting the danger of a Mongol attack.[37] This was probably the famous Mongolian invasion of 1240, and is referred to in song 41.

On another occasion at Langkor he constructed a stūpa in memory of his mother, a project that he commemorates in song 40 and that can probably be dated to 1244. During this time he also placed special offerings into an exceptional representation of Lady Machik Zhama, which was enshrined at Langkor.[38]

Earlier in his life Godrakpa had received some teachings from the renowned Kashmirian master Śākyaśrī. Among the younger Indian scholars accompanying Śākyaśrī during his ten-year stay in Tibet from 1204 to 1214 was the master Vibhūticandra, from whom Godrakpa had also received teachings.[39]

After traveling to Tibet once more on his own, Vibhūticandra settled in Kathmandu, Nepal. During his stay there he received an extraordinary direct transmission of the Six-Branch Yoga of Kālacakra from the great Indian adept Śavaripa. After some consideration Vibhūticandra decided that these special teachings would be of great benefit to many people in Tibet. He questioned a number of Tibetan mendicant yogins in Kathmandu and learned that the most renowned meditation master in Tibet was his former disciple Godrakpa. Vibhūticandra then sent a junior scholar, accompanied by the Tibetan mendicants, to deliver gifts to Godrakpa along with a letter asking him to come to Nepal for the purpose of formally requesting the teachings.[40]

Godrakpa received the invitation at Tingri Langkor and immediately sent a reply and gifts back. He felt that if he went alone to Nepal and received the teaching it would not be of much use to others, but that if Vibhūticandra would come to Tibet there would be widespread benefit. Vibhūticandra accepted the invitation, and Godrakpa provided assistance and many supplies for the trip north.[41]

Four months later a messenger arrived with the news that Vibhūticandra was approaching Gyirong, near the border with Nepal. Godrakpa sent word in all directions that the master would soon be coming to Tingri Langkor and then hurried to Gyirong with offerings to welcome him.[42]

After Vibhūticandra was escorted to Tingri, he bestowed the initiation of Kālacakra, the explanation of the tantra, and the oral instructions for meditation on a large number of Tibetans who had gathered there.[43]

In particular, he taught the special Six-Branch Yoga of Śavaripa to Godrakpa and six other learned men. Vibhūticandra lived at Godrakpa's residence at the Khenpa charnel ground west of Tingri Langkor for two years.

After teaching the Kālacakra three times at Tingri Langkor, Vibhūticandra fell seriously ill. But he was cured by Godrakpa, who used both techniques for removing yogic impediments *(gegs sel)* and medicinal treatments.[44]

Vibhūticandra was very grateful and requested from Godrakpa numerous initiations, textual transmissions, and oral instructions of the Path with the Result, of which Godrakpa was an acknowledged master.[45] This is one of the few instances in which an Indian master is known to have received extensive tantric teachings from a Tibetan.

After Vibhūticandra's return to Nepal, Godrakpa moved about the border regions, staying at many different hermitages, such as Jetsun Milarepa's retreat at Öchung in Drin, which was offered to him, and at Khumpu in

Lower Nyanang, which had been the residence of Lady Machik Zhama's brother, Lord Khumpuwa Chögyal, who had also been a great master of the Path with the Result.[46] At another nearby site, it is said that Godrakpa left footprints in the stone.[47] During this period he received a large offering from the Drukpa Kagyu master, Dharma Lord Götsangpa (Gönpo Dorje, 1189–1258), whose residence was at the Götsang hermitage on Mt. Shrī, not far from Langkor. Götsangpa sent a letter saying that he wished to come in person to meet Godrakpa but that he could not because he was in strict retreat. He therefore requested that Godrakpa write and send him a teaching on generating compassion. Godrakpa sent offerings in return and a letter that said, "In the presence of one like you, other Dharma practitioners are mere reflections. Please continue to maintain your way of life just as before."[48]

Sometime later Godrakpa traveled to the border town of Gyirong to pay homage to the famous image of Avalokiteśvara there, known as the Noble Wati *('Phags pa Wa ti)*. He also distributed a huge quantity of valuables, clothing, grains, and other items among the people of the region. Song 32 was sung during this visit. During his final years Godrakpa continued to travel, renovating temples such as the ancient structure at Dradum (see song 43) and giving many teachings to a vast number of disciples.[49]

When Godrakpa returned to Langkor for the last time, he remarked, "Today the palanquin has served its purpose." He entered his residence, tossed away his cane, and said, "Now I don't need you either." He made a generous distribution of valuables in Langkor and sent a letter to his most important Dharma heir, Gyalwa Yangönpa, who was then in Central Tibet, telling him, "I think I'm not going to stay for more than this eightieth year. Please come when you can." Unfortunately, Yangönpa was unable to come immediately because the roads were blocked by Mongolian troops.[50]

Before his death Godrakpa is said to have uttered many clairvoyant statements, and repeatedly he gave the following advice: "Do everything according to Dharma. Make meditation practice the main thing. Do whatever you can to benefit the Doctrine and living beings."

Then he passed from this world, displaying the manner of the emanation buddha body passing into the taintless expanse of reality. There were countless marvelous omens during the cremation which was led by Gyalwa Yangönpa. Even afterward, those with pure karma, such as Yangönpa, continued to meet Godrakpa in visions and dreams, and to receive his Dharma teachings. For example, one night the master Uyukpa met Godrakpa in a dream, and when he asked for Dharma teachings was told, "Rest the mind without fabrication. Don't meditate with the intellect. Don't think about anything. Heighten the radiance of intrinsic awareness. Sustain ordinary awareness."[51]

After his death Godrakpa's remains were apparently enshrined in his cave at Tingri, and a glass cup that had belonged to him became one of the famous ten holy items of Langkor.[52]

3. The Songs

Only two copies of the collected songs of Godrakpa seem to have survived. Entitled *The Collected Songs of the Adept Godrakpa Who is Peerless in the Three Realms (Khams gsum 'dran bral grub thob ko rag pa'i mgur 'bum),* both texts derive from the same sixteenth century xylograph edition. This collection of songs, which must be one of the smallest of its kind in Tibetan literature, was edited and published by Lhatsun Rinchen Namgyel (1473–1557), who was the most important disciple of Tsang Nyön Heruka (1452–1507), the author/editor of the well-known version of Jetsun Milarepa's biography and collected songs. Lhatsun published a number of works at Tragar Daso *(Brag dkar rta so),* Milarepa's famous retreat near Gyirong.[53] Lhatsun's edition of *The Collected Songs* was probably the first xylograph production of an earlier manuscript. That Godrakpa himself often provides a prose framework for the songs shows that he had an interest and role in the preservation of his own words. This collection of Godrakpa's songs gives the strong impression of being an accurate reflection of what Godrakpa actually sang. The songs have the feel of an original record that has not been polished and standardized by an editor. The verses are very irregular in length, and the spellings are often mere phonetic renderings of classical Tibetan. These same characteristics are noted in early examples of Milarepa's songs, before they were edited, standardized, and polished by Tsang Nyön Heruka.

Like Jetsun Milarepa before him, Godrakpa actually *sang* his songs. He sang in a direct and simple style, using colloquial language and idioms, with a minimal amount of specific technical vocabulary. In the editor's colophon to this collection, Lhatsun Rinchen Namgyel characterizes the songs as "free from mentally fabricated phrases," and as "casual, relaxed, self-emergent, free compositions," which arose in "a primordial, transcendent, self-arisen, unimpeded way." Godrakpa's songs show no literary pretensions, nor do they contain ornate poetic imagery. In some places they are terse and sharp in tone, while in others they are lyrical and filled with allusions to the surrounding landscape and wildlife. In only three songs (1, 6 and 38) does Godrakpa even mention specific teachings or texts. In several others he incorporates verses from Milarepa (song 4), the Kagyu master Lingchen Repa (1128–88; song 21), and the Indian adept Śavaripa (songs 32 and 43), but without identifying them as such. Song 3 is closely based on one of Milarepa's songs, and song 38 contains several lines inspired by another of the earlier master's works.[54] Godrakpa's audience would have recognized these lines. This same sort of borrowing has continued to be commonplace in Tibetan literature and is seen as an acknowledgment of the source of the author's inspiration.

Lhatsun Rinchen Namgyel

Only song 2 presupposes specific esoteric knowledge on the part of the listener—in this case a familiarity with the structure and teachings of the Path with the Result. Most of the songs would have been comprehensible to any Dharma practitioner of the time, and many could have been understood by nonpractitioners as well. Local audiences would have recognized place names, and practitioners in Godrakpa's environment would have known that the "Great Brahmin" and the "Indian Lord" referred to the Indian adepts Saraha and Phadampa Sangye.

More can be learned about the nature of the speaker from the style and content of these songs than from any other source. For example, Godrakpa's frequent references to himself as a "beggar" are to be taken literally. He did wander the barren wastelands of western Tibet as a beggar-yogin, as had his own teacher Nyö Chögyi Ziji, and as had Jetsun Milarepa before them.[55] Other songs provide unique insights into Godrakpa's character. Especially noteworthy is the preface to song 8, where he allows an extraordinary glimpse into his determination to meditate despite serious illness and comes to see the illness itself as indispensable to his practice. Song 2 is an exceptionally honest and vivid description of the difficulties he encountered during a long meditation retreat. Other songs also relate to specific events during his life.

Godrakpa expressed in his songs what he emphasized in his life—a no-nonsense approach to the practice of meditation. He speaks repeatedly of impermanence, imminent death, and the danger of wasting time. He stresses the importance of recognizing that true reality lies within each person by making reference to intrinsic awareness, the realization of the Great Seal, and the buddha body of reality that is only to be found within, beyond the reaches of jargon and technical terminology. Finally Godrakpa speaks of his own confidence, an unshakable conviction that allows him to state that he has nothing more to ask about the truth, even if Buddha Vajradhara himself were available to answer questions.

Each of Godrakpa's songs creates a certain effect in the listener or reader. Listen to him speak about death:

> This death of ours is like the shadow of a bird in flight.
> The Dharma of a sudden descent is taught,
> but no one is energetic toward the next life,
> and I haven't seen singing a song help. (song 14)
>
> Striving—striving for the aims of this life,
> the body aging and approaching death wasn't noticed.
> It's too late to practice the divine Dharma. (song 26)

Closely linked with an awareness of death is a certainty of impermanence and the fact that present opportunities are fleeting:

> This youthful vitality is like a flower in spring.
> The Dharma of fading impermanence is taught,

but the young don't practice the divine Dharma,
and I haven't seen singing a song help. (song 14)

To the serum of youth, which is like a flower,
the young are attached like witless bees.
Not recognizing this is impermanent and fading,
those who wander in endless lower realms
get so exhausted. (song 18)

Contemplation of these subjects produces a feeling of disillusionment and weariness with mundane life in saṃsāra, coupled with a determination to make good use of the present, unique opportunities. To this end it is also necessary to understand the relationship between actions and their results, or the law of karma:

Cause and result are like the seeds
of the six kinds of living beings.
Watch how what is planted ripens.

Some engage in the causes of suffering;
some abide in the results of suffering.
There's no happiness in this saṃsāra. (song 16)

Although thoroughly disillusioned with saṃsāra, a practitioner of the Mahāyāna remains deeply concerned about the welfare of others and is motivated to achieve enlightenment in order to remove them from suffering. Godrakpa's songs emphasize the importance of renunciation and solitary meditation. An ordinary, mundane lifestyle is cluttered and busy. To be able to help others we have to recognize the way things really are, the nature of our own minds. This is the essential point of most of Godrakpa's songs, sometimes expressed in a refrain, sometimes in a single line:

Mind watching mind,
that's this beggar's experience of practice.

Cherishing others more than myself,
that's this beggar's application of practice. (song 38)

Mind insubstantial like empty sky;
thoughts unestablished like breezes in space. (song 36)

When I went to meditate in mountain-range solitude,
I briefly encountered realization of mind itself. (song 17)

The realization of the nature of mind is referred to by many names, one of which is the Great Seal. Although this term is usually associated with the teachings of the Kagyu lineages, it is used in all the tantric traditions to indicate a state of utter simplicity, a naked experience of the way things really are:

Looking out at the external objects of the six groups,[56]
I saw them to be the magical display of birthless mind.

Looking in at the internal, intrinsic awareness of mind,
there was the groundless, rootless nature of mind that is
forever empty.

Examining the attentive, aware mind in between,
incidental thoughts free themselves.

An inner understanding such as this
is the view of the Great Seal. (song 6)

When incidental thoughts arise,
recognize the awareness of the moment.

Leave the mind in an unfabricated, fresh state.
The way things really are dawns from within. (song 35)

These verses point to an experience, yet true experience for the meditator is inexpressible. Unshakable confidence is born when one experiences meaning beyond the reach of descriptive words:

If all phenomena aren't understood to be mind,
even with all these inconceivable expressions,

the end of words will never be reached.
Get used to the essential meaning. (song 5)

When he presented the meaning of the Great Seal,
the oral instructions were like water poured into water.
Even if great Vajradhara came,
I'd surely have nothing to ask about the meaning. (song 4)

To overanalyze statements such as these would destroy the spirit of the songs. Let the reader listen to Godrakpa's words with a mind open to the advice of a person who lived what he taught:

I'm this yogi whose mindstream
 has been refined with both love and compassion.
I give advice with kind intentions.
Please listen with a sympathetic mind. (song 16)

NOTES TO THE INTRODUCTION

1 These lines have been translated from the quotation in Sa chen Kun dga' snying po, *Lam*, 70. In Sa chen Kun dga' snying po, *Gzhung*, 195, the author of the quotation is identified as Lady Lhajema *(Jo mo Lha rje ma)*, which is an epithet of Machik Zhama *(Ma gcig Zha ma)*.

2 See Kapstein (1996), 276–80, for a brief discussion of the eight major systems. In categorizing these surviving Tibetan traditions of spiritual instruction, Kongdrul was following an eightfold classification system that had already been in use for centuries: (1) the Ancient Translation Tradition *(Snga 'gyur rnying ma)*, (2) the Tradition of Precepts and Instructions *(Bka' gdams pa)*, (3) the Tradition of the Path with the Result *(Lam 'bras)*, (4) the Tradition of the Transmitted Precepts of Marpa *(Mar pa bka' brgyud)*, (5) the Tradition of the Transmitted Precepts of the Shang Valley *(Shangs pa bka' brgyud)*, (6) the traditions of Pacification *(Zhi byed)* and Severance *(Gcod)*, (7) the Tradition of the Vajrayoga *(Rdo rje rnal 'byor)* of the Kālacakra tantra, and (8) the Propitiation and Attainment of the Three Adamantine States *(Rdo rje gsum gyi bsnyen sgrub)*, also connected with the Kālacakra tantra.

3 The dates used here for Marpa *(Mar pa)* and Phadampa Sangye *(Pha dam pa Sangs rgyas)* and elsewhere for Milarepa *(Mi la ras pa)* are those established by Rikdzin Tsewang Norbu (*Rig 'dzin Tshe dbang nor bu*, 1698–1755) in his study of the dates and chronologies in the lives of the early Kagyu *(Bka' brgyud)* masters. See Tshe dbang nor bu, *Mar*. I am preparing a translation of this text for future publication.

4 In Roerich (1976), 726–27, Godrakpa's dates are given as 1182–1261. Mang thos Klu sgrub rgya mtsho, *Bstan*, 143, questions these, gives the earlier birth date of 1170, and states that Godrakpa lived to the age of eighty (1249). The dates 1170–1249 are certainly preferable. Godrakpa's most important disciple was the Kagyu master Yangönpa (*Yang dgon pa Rgyal mtshan dpal bzang po*, 1213–58). Just before his death Godrakpa sent for Yangönpa. Since Yangönpa is known to have died in 1258, and was obviously still alive at the time of Godrakpa's passing, and

presided over his funeral ceremonies, the earlier set of dates for Godrakpa are a better choice. See both Shes rab mgon, *Chos*, 9a, and Rin chen ldan, *Rin*, 44. Cf. van der Kuijp (1994), 186.

5 Lady Machik Zhama was a disciple of both the Indian master Phadampa Sangye, who brought the teachings of Severence and Pacification to Tibet, and of the master Sedön Kunrig (*Se ston Kun rig*, 1025–1122), who was the main disciple of the great Drokmi Lotsawa *('Brog mi Lo tsā ba)*, the first Tibetan teacher of the Path with the Result. See Stearns (forthcoming) for my translation and study of the earliest biographical materials concerning Machik Zhama, as well as for general information on the Path with the Result and its early history in Tibet.

6 For a discussion of this tradition, see Stearns (1996).

7 See 'Gos Lo tsā ba, *Deb*, vol. 2, 852, and Roerich (1976), 727.

8 Mang thos Klu sgrub rgya mtsho, *Bstan*, 143.

9 See note 44.

10 See Thu'u bkwan Blo bzang Chos kyi nyi ma, *Thu'u*, 233.

11 See Kun dga' grol mchog, *Khrid*, 329. This text by Godrakpa does not seem to have survived.

12 For example, Jonang Tāranātha (1575–1635) stated that the oral instructions of Godrakpa's Path with the Result were still being transmitted during his time, and that all the reading transmissions for Godrakpa's tradition were also extant. See Tāranātha, *Stag*, 573. The Fifth Dalai Lama, Ngawang Lozang Gyantso (*Ngag dbang blo bzang rgya mtsho*, 1617–82), also received the transmission of the only one of Godrakpa's works on the Path with the Result now available, although he seems to have included it among the compositions of the great Sakya master Lama Dampa Sönam Gyaltsen (*Bla ma dam pa Bsod nams rgyal mtshan*, 1312–75), which are collectively known as *The Black Volume (Pod nag)*. See Ngag dbang blo bzang rgya mtsho, *Zab*, vol. 1, 454. The presently available edition of *The Black Volume* does not include Godrakpa's text. This confusion of authorship is probably due to the fact that Godrakpa's name was also Sönam Gyaltsen. Also see note 34.

13 Although the number eighteen is perhaps the most common, further classifications were also made, to the point that there were some twenty-four different lineages. For example, see 'Jam mgon A mes zhabs, *Yongs*, 173–76.

14 Ngor chen, *Lam*, 114–18, is the earliest source to discuss the different lineages, and he places Godrakpa's Path with the Result in the "female transmission." See Ngor chen, *Lam*, 115.1 and 116.3. On the other hand, some two hundred years later 'Jam mgon A mes zhabs, *Yongs*, 175, classifies Godrakpa's system among the "combined transmissions."

15 See the section on Godrakpa's life, and Stearns (1996), 147–49, for information on Vibhūticandra's teachings of the Six-Branch Yoga. In this connection, E. Gene Smith has also stated that the origins of the Bodong *(Bo dong)* tradition go back to Godrakpa. See Smith (1969b), 1, note 1.

16 I am grateful to Leonard van der Kuijp for a copy of the biography by Sherab Gön *(Shes rab mgon)*, which is described in van der Kuijp (1994), 185–86. The author of Godrakpa's biography can now be identified as the Sherab Gön who was the author of several texts found in the collected works of Godrakpa's disciple, Gyalwa Yangönpa. This Sherab Gön studied with disciples of Yangönpa and was a practitioner of the Drukpa Kagyu *('Brug pa Bka' brgyud)* tradition in the late thirteenth century. See Roerich (1976), 695–96, for a short sketch of his life. Sherab Gön refers to himself as a "beggar" in the colophons of both the biography of Godrakpa (using the term *sprang po*) and a text in Yangönpa's works (using the term *ldom bu pa*). See Shes rab mgon, *Chos*, 10a, and *Ri*, 9.

17 See song 1, and Shes rab mgon, *Chos*, 1b–2a.

18 According to Shes rab mgon, *Chos*, 2b, during this period Godrakpa also received teachings from the famous Indian master of Kashmir, the great Śākyaśrī (1140s–1225?). Since it is established that Śākyaśrī was in Tibet from 1204 to 1214, Godrakpa's meeting must have occurred considerably later in his life.

19 Shes rab mgon, *Chos*, 2a–b.

20 Shes rab mgon, *Chos*, 2a–b.

21 Shes rab mgon, *Chos*, 3a.

22 See also Shes rab mgon, *Chos*, 3a.

23 See also Shes rab mgon, *Chos*, 3b.

24 This is a reference to a type of experience that can arise during the practice of tantric yoga. In particular, according to the teachings of the Path with the Result,

when the vital winds and mind *(rlung sems)* gather in specific channel locations in the subtle vajra body of the practitioner, experiences of being born in different realms may arise. These experiences actually purify the causes for future rebirth in those realms. However, if the experiences persist for too long, they can cause obstacles on the spiritual path. Specific remedies are therefore provided for resolving them. In his treatise on the Path with the Result, Godrakpa describes the experience of being born in the hell realm and presents the corresponding remedies. See Ko brag pa, *Lam*, 552, and 557–58.

25 The significance of Lady Lakṣmīṅkarā's appearance is probably linked to the fact that one of Godrakpa's main meditations was Vajravārāhī. It is known that he received from the master Semikpa the transmission of the practices of the form of this goddess that had been transmitted through Lakṣmīṅkarā. This is known as the Jal Tradition of Vajravārāhī *(Dpyal lugs phag mo)*, and is a form of Vajravārāhī holding her own severed head.

26 Godrakpa's teacher can be identified as Nyö Chögyi Ziji (*Gnyos Chos kyi gzi brjid*, 1164–1224) of Kharak *(Kha rag)*, who was a master of the teachings of the Path with the Result in the lineage of Lady Machik Zhama, which he had received from Nyang Gyalpo Trak of Mönkar *(Smon mkhar ba Nyang Rgyal po grags)*. See Ngor chen, *Lam*, 116.4. Nyö was also one of the chief disciples of the Drigung Kagyu *('Bri gung bka' brgyud)* master Jikden Gönpo (*'Jig rten mgon po*, 1143–1217). See Anonymous, *Kha*, 31–39, and Jñānavajra, *Gnyos*, for the story of Nyö's life.

27 Shes rab mgon, *Chos*, 4b.

28 Shes rab mgon, *Chos*, 4b–5a.

29 See Tāranātha, *Myang*, 148, for the location of Godrak *(Ko brag)*.

30 See Ngor chen, *Lam*, 116.2–3; Anonymous, *Kha*, 36–37; and Jñānavajra, *Gnyos*, 101. I am indebted to Hubert Decleer and Franz-Karl Ehrhard for a copy of Jñānavajra's work.

31 See Ngor chen, *Lam*, 116.2–3, and Shes rab mgon, *Chos*, 5a.

32 The cave of Rasa Chuphuk *(Ra sa Chu phug)* is perhaps the same as Godrakpa's cave, called Chumik Marsöl *(Chu mig dmar gsol)*, located on the summit of the northern mountain of Setrak *(Bse brag)* in Upper Nyang. See Tāranātha, *Myang*, 121.

33 The best source on this is Ngor chen, *Lam*, 116.4. 'Jam dbyangs Mkhyen brtse'i dbang phyug, *Gsang*, 76b–77a, and 'Jam mgon A mes zhabs, *Yongs*, 169–70, basi-

cally repeat the information in Ngor chen, with less detail and a few additions.

34 Only one of the many texts written by Godrakpa explaining the practice of the Path with the Result is presently available. This text is an explanation of the Path with the Result in the tradition of Lady Machik Zhama and focuses primarily on the elimination of obstacles to meditation. It is the only text that is extant on the meditation practices of the Path with the Result in the Zhama tradition. See Ko brag pa, *Lam*, which was written at the isolated site of Chuphuk *(Dben gnas Chu phug).* Also see Stearns (1996), 141, n. 51, and 144, n. 60. As discussed in note 12, it is curious that the Fifth Dalai Lama lists a text which seems to perfectly fit the description of this work by Godrakpa among the texts in the collection of *The Black Volume (Pod nag)* composed by the Sakya master Sönam Gyaltsen.

35 See Shes rab mgon, *Chos*, 6a, and Rin chen ldan, *Rin*, 41–44.

36 Yangönpa's reverence for Godrakpa, and his practice of the Path with the Result, are frequently mentioned in his own spiritual songs. See for example, Yang dgon pa, *Rgyal*, 207–12, 221, 230, 238, 242, 249, 259, 262, 279, etc. It is of special interest that Yangönpa also sought out the great Sakya Paṇḍita and received from him the complete transmission of the Path with the Result according to the Sakya tradition. Although Yangönpa's songs indicate that his practice of the Path with the Result was according to Godrakpa's teachings in the lineage of Lady Machik Zhama, his masterful treatise on the state of the subtle "vajra body" *(rdo rje'i lus)* represents a synthesis of material received from his four most important teachers. In addition to Godrakpa and Sakya Paṇḍita, the other two were Drigung Jen Nga (*'Bri gung Spyan snga,* 1175–1255) and Götsangpa Gönpo Dorje (*Rgod tshang pa Mgon po rdo rje,* 1189–1258). Like his teacher Godrakpa, Yangönpa also stated that he had actually seen the channels and the forms of the vital winds circulating in the subtle vajra body. At several points in his text, which is entitled *A Hidden Explanation of the Vajra Body (Rdo rje lus kyi sbas bshad),* Yangönpa refers specifically to the opinions of Sakya Paṇḍita and to the Path with the Result. According to the late Dezhung Rinpoche (1906–87), the exceptional Sakya master Tsarchen Losel Gyantso (*Tshar chen Blo gsal rgya mtsho,* 1502–66) later incorporated large sections of Yangönpa's text into his own explanation of the subtle body. See Tshar chen, *Zab.* A comparison of the two texts shows that this is in fact the case. For the last 450 years, Tsarchen's text has been the definitive exposition for the Sakya tradition. Thus some of the teachings of both Godrakpa and Sakya Paṇḍita were channeled into the mainstream Sakya Path with the Result tradition through the writings of Yangönpa. For Yangönpa's studies with Sakya Paṇḍita, see Rin chen ldan, *Rin*, 76–78. Another important work by Yangönpa that combined teachings such as the Path with the Result with other lineages is the *Three Cycles of Mountain Dharma (Ri chos skor gsum).*

37 See Roerich (1976), 679.

38 Shes rab mgon, *Chos,* 6a–b.

39 See Stearns (1996), 141–45, from which the following account has been summarized.

40 See Tāranātha, *Rdo,* 483, and especially Padma gar dbang, *Zab,* 226a–27a, who quotes both Vibhūticandra's letter and Godrakpa's reply.

41 See Tāranātha, *Rdo,* 483. Grönbold (1982), 340, mistakenly states that Godrakpa invited the master Śākyaśrī to Tibet.

42 Padma gar dbang, *Zab,* 27a–b.

43 Padma gar dbang, *Zab,* 27b.

44 Padma gar dbang, *Zab,* 27b–28a. Godrakpa is most well known in the literature of the Path with the Result for his expertise in techniques for the removal of impediments *(gegs sel)* during the practice of yoga. He is also said to have gained incredible realization on the basis of his practice of the Path with the Result and the Six-Branch Yoga, and is known to have written texts combining these two systems of tantric practice. In addition to the traditional techniques for removal of impediments according to the Path with the Result, Godrakpa wrote many texts about previously unknown techniques that were revealed to him when he directly perceived the network of energy pathways in the vajra body during meditation. As mentioned above, the most famous of his works is the *Gegs sel ha dmigs rgya mtsho.* He also authored a text on the elimination of illnesses and demonic influences *(nad gdon dbyung ba'i man ngag).* See Ngor chen, *Lam,* 116.

45 Padma gar dbang, *Zab,* 28a. Shes rab mgon, *Chos,* 7a, also verifies that Vibhūticandra received some teachings from Godrakpa, as do several other sources.

46 Shes rab mgon, *Chos,* 7a, gives the spelling Öchung *('Os chung).* The spelling Omchung *('Om chung)* is found in Bstan 'dzin Chos kyi blo gros, *Gsang,* 34, who provides the information that Nyö Gyalwa Lhanangpa *(Gnyos Rgyal ba Lha nang pa)* stayed in this place after Milarepa, and then Godrakpa lived there. Nyö Gyalwa Lhanangpa is another name used for Nyö Chögyi Ziji, from whom Godrakpa received the Path with the Result teachings of the Zhama tradition. A short climb down to the east from this site leads to another cave where Godrakpa lived, which was thus known as Godrak Cave *(Ko brag phug).* Both the Omchung Cave and the

Godrak Cave are still remembered today as places where Godrakpa stayed. Personal communication from Andy Quintman, 6/5/99.

47 Bstan 'dzin Chos kyi blo gros, *Gsang*, 42. Village elders of the area still identify a pair of footprints as Godrakpa's. Personal communication from Andy Quintman, 6/5/99. Bstan 'dzin Chos kyi blo gros, *Gsang*, 48 and 50, mentions that Godrakpa also spent time in the large cave where Jetsun Milarepa had subdued many hostile demons, and which is thus famed as the Düdül Phukmoche *(Bdud 'dul phug mo che)*, the "Great Cave of Demon Subjugation." For a translation of these passages, see Huber (1997), 262–63.

48 Shes rab mgon, *Chos*, 7b.

49 The ancient temple of Dradum in Tsang *(Btsang Pra thum*, which is also spelled *Gtsang [S]pra [b]dun)* was one of the *mtha' 'dul* temples built in the seventh century to suppress the hostile geomantic forces in the Tibetan landscape. See Aris (1979), 23, and 294, n. 49, etc. See Roerich (1976), 727–28, for a list of Godrakpa's important disciples.

50 See Shes rab mgon, *Chos*, 9a, and Rin chen ldan, *Rin*, 44.

51 For both this and the quote in the previous paragraph, see Shes rab mgon, *Chos*, 9b. The master Uyukpa had earlier invited Godrakpa to teach at the monastery of Tashi Khangmar *(Bkra shis khang dmar)*. See Shes rab mgon, *Chos*, 5a, and song 11. Uyukpa Rikpey Senge (*'U yug pa Rigs pa'i seng ge*, d. 1253) was the foremost disciple of Sakya Paṇḍita in the field of epistemology *(pramāṇa, tshad ma)*.

52 See Aziz (1979), 37–38. I am understanding the term *ku-dum* used by Aziz to be a phonetic rendering of the Tibetan spelling of *sku gdung*, the honorific term for physical remains. A portion of Godrakpa's bones are also counted among the holy objects enshrined in the famous Great Cave of Demon Subjugation *(Bdud 'dul phug mo che)* in Labchi. See Bstan 'dzin Chos kyi blo gros, *Gsang*, 63. At the end of the sixteenth century, Tāranātha mentions visiting Langkor and presenting offerings to a special image of Godrakpa. See Tāranātha, *Rgyal*, 178.

53 See Smith (1969), 25–31, for information on Lhatsun and his publishing work at Tragar Daso, and especially 12–16 on style and orthographical peculiarities. A number of important unpublished works, some authored and some edited by Lhatsun, are languishing in the microfilm collection of the Nepal-German Manuscript Preservation Project.

54 See Rus pa'i rgyan can (= Gtsang smyon He ru ka), *Rnal*, 272 and 436–37, and Chang (1962), vol. 1, 100 and 280–81.

55 From the age of twenty-nine (1193), Nyö Chögyi Ziji wandered east into Kham *(Khams)*, living as a beggar. See Anonymous, *Kha*, 34. In addition to frequently referring to himself as a beggar *(sprang po)* in his songs, Godrakpa also refers to himself as a Buddhist mendicant monk *(shakya'i dge slong ldom bu ba)* in his preface to song 9.

56 This is a reference to the apparently external objects of the six groups of the consciousnesses: sight, hearing, smell, taste, body, and mind.

THE COLLECTED SONGS OF THE ADEPT

GODRAKPA

WHO IS PEERLESS
IN THE THREE REALMS

Vajra Dhvaja

།།ན་མོ་གུ་རུ་དེ་ཝ་ཌཱ་ཀི་ནི།

ཐོས་བསམ་རྟོགས་པ་མངོན་གྱུར་ཆོས་སྐུའི་ངང་། །བྱམས་དང་སྙིང་རྗེས་འགྲོ་ལ་གཟུགས་སྐུར་བཞེངས།
།བརྟུལ་ཞུགས་སྤྱོད་པས་འགྲོ་ཀུན་སྨིན་གྲོལ་འགོད། །རྫུ་འཕྲུལ་མཐར་ཕྱིན་ཀོ་རག་རྗེ་ལ་འདུད།

།རྗེ་རྣལ་འབྱོར་གྱི་དབང་ཕྱུག་ཀོ་རག་པ་ཞེས་བྱ་བ། མཚན་ཡོངས་སུ་གྲགས་པ་དེ་ཉིད་ཀྱི་གསུང་ནས་བྱོན་པའི་མགུར་མ་མཐའ་ཡས་ཀྱང་རག་བསྡུས་གཅིག་བརྗོད་པར་བྱའོ།

Namo Guru Deva Ḍākinī

I bow to Lord Godrak, who actualized the realization of learning
and contemplation, and from the state of the buddha body
of reality arose in the buddha body of form with love and
compassion for the world,
Who brought all living beings to maturation and liberation
through deliberate behavior, and who reached the
perfection of magical abilities.

The songs that emerged from the speech of the one known by the name "Lord Godrakpa, Master of Yogins," were infinite, and so just an approximate collection will be presented here.

༡

།དེ་ལ་སྔོན་གྱི་བག་ཆགས་སད་པའི་རྣམ་ཐར་མགུར་དུ་བཞེངས་པ།།

།།ན་མོ་ར་ཏྣ་གུ་རུ།

བདག་དང་པོ་ཆུང་དུ་བྱིས་པ་ནས། །བྱ་བློ་ཆོས་ལས་མི་བརྡོག་པས།
།སྦྱངས་པའི་ཡོན་ཏན་མི་ཤེས་ནས། །སད་ཀྱུའི་ཕྱོགས་སུ་འཁྱམ་དུ་ཕྱིན།

།སློབ་དཔོན་ལྡོང་དང་ཏུག་གིས་མཇལ། །ཕྱག་རྟེན་དུ་ཤེས་རབ་ཆེན་པོ་ཕུལ།
།གདམ་ངག་ཏུ་སྣྲ་སྣྲོ་མཚོན་ཆ་གནང་། །ཡི་གེ་ལ་མཁས་པའི་དོན་ཤེས་ནས།
།ཡོན་ཏན་གྱི་གཞི་མ་དེ་ནས་ཐེངས།

།དེ་ནས་ལོ་འགའ་ལོན་ཙ་ན། །དད་པ་གཏིང་ནས་སྐྱེས་ལགས་པས།
།ལྷ་འཁོར་གྱི་ཕྱོགས་སུ་འཁྱམ་ཏུ་ཕྱིན།

།སློབ་དཔོན་བླ་མ་དང་ཏུག་གིས་མཇལ། །ཕྱག་རྟེན་དུ་དད་པ་བརྟན་པོ་ཕུལ།
།སྡིག་སྦྱོང་དོན་ཡོད་ཞགས་པ་ཞུས། །ཡིད་དམ་ཕྱག་ན་རྡོ་རྗེ་གནང་།
།རང་ལུས་ལྷ་སྐུའི་དོན་གོ་བས། །ཐ་མལ་གྱི་སྣང་བ་དེ་ནས་འགྱུར།

།དེ་ནས་ལོ་འགའ་ལོན་ཙམ་ན། །འཁོར་བས་སྐྱོ་བ་སྐྱེས་ལགས་ནས།
།རྒྱ་གར་ཡུལ་དུ་ཆས་ལགས་པས། །དྲིན་ཅན་ཕ་རྒན་གྱིས་མ་བཏང་ནས།
།སྟ་ནང་གྱི་ཕྱོགས་སུ་འཁྱམ་དུ་ཕྱིན།

1

Sung as a biography in song about the awakening of previous propensities:

Namo Ratna Guru

From when I was first a small child
   I had no thought to do anything but Dharma.
Ignorant of the good qualities of learning
   I wandered off in the direction of Segyu.

Briefly I met the teacher Dong,
and offered great intelligence as a gift.
He granted *The Weapon to Open the Door of Speech*
   as an oral instruction.
I understood the significance of skill in letters,
and from that the foundation of good qualities was laid.

Then when several years had passed
   there was a deep birth of faith,
so I wandered off in the direction of Langkor.

Briefly I met the teacher and master,
and offered firm faith as a gift.
I requested Amoghapāśa for purification of sins.
He granted Vajrapāṇi as the chosen deity.
When I understood the truth of my body as a divine
   buddha body,
ordinary appearances were thereafter transformed.

Then when several years had passed
   I was wearied by saṃsāra
      and started off for the land of India.
But my kind old father wouldn't release me,
so I wandered off in the direction of Nyanang.

།བདག་དམ་པ་ཆོས་ཀྱི་སྒོར་ཞུགས་ནས། །སྒྲོ་སྦྲམ་གྱི་སྟེང་དུ་མ་བསྡད་ཅིང་།
།དྲིགས་པ་ཁྲུ་བརྒྱབ་མ་བགྱིས་པར། །ཐོས་པས་ཕྱིའི་སྒྲོ་འདོགས་བཅད།

།ཆོས་དཀའ་ལས་བྱས་ནས་འདི་ཚོ་ཞུས།

།ཕ་དྲིན་ཅན་གྱི་སྤྲུལ་སྐུ་ཞང་སྟོན་ལ། །དབང་བཞི་རྫོགས་པའི་རིམ་པ་ཞུས།
།བསླབ་བྱ་སྐྱབས་འགྲོ་སེམས་བསྐྱེད་ཞུས། །ལག་ལེན་གསང་སྔགས་མ་རྒྱུད་ཞུས།
།བསྒོམ་བྱ་ལམ་གྱི་རིམ་པ་ཞུས། །ལམ་ཁྲིར་ཕ་རོལ་ཕྱིན་པ་ཞུས།
།ཉམས་ལེན་ཕྱག་རྒྱ་ཆེན་པོ་ཞུས། །སྒྲུབ་ཐབས་མི་གཡོ་མགོན་པོ་ཞུས།
།བརྗོད་བྱེད་མངོན་པ་གནས་གསུམ་ཞུས། །གྲུབ་མཐའ་དབུ་མ་ཆེན་པོ་ཞུས།
།བསོའི་རིག་པ་ཅེར་མཐོང་ཞུས། །ལྷ་སྒོམ་མདོའ་ཧ་སྐོར་གསུམ་ཞུས།
།གདམ་ངག་ཀོར་ཚོ་ཀོར་ཚོ་ཞུས།

།བླ་འབོར་གྱི་སློབ་དཔོན་བླ་མ་ལ། །སྙན་རྒྱུད་རིགས་འཛིན་བཅུ་པ་ཞུས།
།ངོ་སྤྲོད་རྒན་མོ་འཛུབ་ཚུགས་ཞུས། །ལག་ལེན་རྫོགས་ཆེན་དམར་ཁྲིད་ཞུས།

།རྒྱ་ཕུབས་ཀྱི་སློབ་དཔོན་རྗེ་སྲས་ལ། །བཀའ་ཆོས་རྫོགས་པ་ཆེན་པོ་ཞུས།
།ཡང་སྙིང་ཤེས་རབ་སྙིང་པོ་ཞུས།

After I entered the gate of the excellent Dharma,
I didn't dwell in agitated states of mind
  or indulge in arrogance,
and outer doubts were removed through learning.

After undergoing hardship for the Dharma
  I made these requests:

From my spiritual father,
the kind emanation buddha body Zhangdön,
I requested the stages of the complete four initiations.
I requested the precepts for taking refuge
  and awakening the enlightenment mind.
I requested as practice the mother tantras of secret mantra.
I requested the Stages of the Path to be meditated on.
I requested the Perfections to be carried on the path.
I requested the Great Seal as the practice.
I requested the method for realization of Acalanātha.
I requested the three topics of Abhidharma to be taught.
I requested the Great Middle Way as philosophical tenet.
I requested *So's Naked Perception of Intrinsic Awareness.*
I requested *The Dohā Trilogy* as view and meditation.
I requested various minor oral instructions.

From the teacher and master of Langkor
  I requested as an aural transmission *The Tenth Upholder*
    of Intrinsic Awareness.
I requested as an introduction *The Finger Pointed*
  at the Old Woman.
I requested as practice the practical instructions
  of the Great Perfection.

From Josey the teacher of Gyaphub
  I requested the Great Perfection as a Dharma teaching.
I requested *The Heart Sūtra* as the quintessence.

།རྒྱན་མུར་གྱི་སློབ་དཔོན་གཉོས་སྟོན་ལ། །ཕ་རོལ་ཕྱིན་པ་སྙན་རྒྱུད་ཞུས།

།ས་གོར་གྱི་སློབ་དཔོན་སྙལ་སྒོམ་ལ། །གདམ་ངག་ཟབ་མོ་རྒྱན་གཙོད་ཞུས།
།བསྙན་བསྲུངས་ནག་པོ་ཙི་ཏ་ཞུས།

།དྲིན་ཅན་ཁ་རག་གཙང་པ་ལ། །གདམ་ངག་ཟབ་མོ་ལམ་འབྲས་ཞུས།

།སློན་མཁར་གྱི་སློབ་དཔོན་ཤེར་ཚུལ་ལ། །ལག་ལེན་དབང་གི་ཆུ་བོ་ཞུས།

།ཨེ་མ་ཧོ།།
སི་ཧི་ཕ་ལ་ཧོ།།

ཨྠི

From Nyödön the teacher of Gyenmur
  I requested the aural transmission of the Perfections.

From Nyelgom the teacher of Sagor
  I requested the profound oral instructions of Cutting the Stream.
I requested Nakpo Tsita, the protector of the Doctrine.

From the kind Kharak Tsangpa
  I requested the profound oral instructions of the Path with the Result.

From Shertsul the teacher of Mönkhar
  I requested the stream of initiation as the practice.

E Ma Ho
Siddhi Phala Ho

Iti

༣

།ན་མོ་གུ་རུ།

ཁོ་བོ་སྤྲང་པོ་དགེ་ཆཞེས་བདག། འབྲོག་ལ་ཕྱི་གངས་ཀྱི་ར་བ་རུ།
།རང་ཅིག་ཕུར་ཉམས་སུ་བླངས་པ་ལས། །ནང་གི་སྐྱེ་ཚུལ་འདི་ལྟར་བྱུང་།

།ང་འདི་ལྷ་བུ་རུ་ཡོངས་པ་ལས། །རྒྱུད་ཐ་མལ་དུ་བསྡད་དུ་མ་ཕོམ་ནས།
།མི་རྟག་པས་བློ་སྣ་ནང་དུ་བསྡུངས། །འཁོར་བའི་ཆོས་ལ་སྐྱོ་བ་སྐྱེས།
།སྣང་བ་རྨི་ལམ་སྒྱུ་མར་མཐོང་། །བརྩོན་འགྲུས་ལུས་སེམས་ལ་གཟན་པར་བྱུང་།

།རིག་པ་བཞུར་ནས་བསྒོམས་ལགས་པས། །ཁམས་འདུས་པ་ཉམས་ཀྱི་སྣང་བ་ལ།
།ངོ་མཚར་འཆར་ལུགས་ཅི་ཡང་བྱུང་།

།ས་རྡོ་མི་རུ་མཐོང་པ་བྱུང་། །རྩི་ཤིང་མཆོད་དུ་མཐོང་པ་བྱུང་།

།སྣང་ཡོག་ཆེན་པོ་དེ་ཙམ་ན། །རེས་འགའ་སྙིང་རླུང་འཇུག་གམ་མནོས།
།རེས་འགའ་སྨྱོ་ནས་འགྲོ་འམ་མནོས། །ལུས་འདོམ་གང་གྲུ་བཞི་ལ་བདེ་བ་མེད།
།སྙིང་ཡང་མ་དགའ་ཆ་མ་ཆེ། །ཁམས་ཀྱང་མི་བདེ་ཚབ་མ་ཚུབ།
།ནད་དང་གདོན་གྱི་རྟོག་པར་སོང་། །ཡར་ང་ལས་སྡུག་པ་མེད་དོ་མནོས།

།ཉིང་འཛིན་ངོ་བོས་མ་ཟིན་པས། །འཆར་ལུགས་ལམ་དུ་མ་སློངས་པས།
།རྒྱུན་དཀའི་རླུང་པོ་ལས་བྱེད་འདྲ། །ཁམས་འདུས་པ་དང་པོའི་འཆར་ལུགས་ལགས།

2

Namo Guru

I'm beggar, I'm spiritual friend.
Practicing alone in the glacial enclosure of Drok Labchi
  an inner birth happened like this.

When practicing in this way,
with no opportunity for the mindstream to stay ordinary,
the mind was reined in with impermanence,
weariness with the phenomena of saṃsāra arose,
appearances were seen as dream and illusion,
body and mind were dominated by diligence.

When intrinsic awareness was exposed in meditation,
in the experiential appearances of the gathering of the constituents
  wonders dawned in every way.

Earth and rocks were seen as human beings,
trees were seen as weapons.

At that great reversal of appearances,
sometimes I wondered if I were afflicted by depression,
sometimes I wondered if I were going insane.
No comfort in the cramped dungeon of the body,
heart not at ease, but fluttering about,
health also sickly and shaky,
thoughts of illness and demons.
In general I thought none suffered more than I.

Not identified as the essence of meditative concentration,
the way things dawned wasn't taken as the path.
Like the action of the winter wind,
the first gathering of the constituents dawned.

།དུས་དང་གནས་སྐབས་དེ་ཙམ་ན། །མ་བདེ་བ་ལ་ཞུ་ས་མེད།
།སྐྱོན་རྣམས་བྱུང་ཡང་གགས་སེལ་མེད། །ཡོན་ཏན་བྱུང་ཡང་བོགས་འདོན་མེད།

།བློ་ཁ་ནང་དུ་བཟློག་པ་ལས། །བླ་མའི་གདམ་ངག་ཏུར་གྱིས་དྲན།
།བྱང་རྒྱལ་གྱི་སྤྱོད་པ་མ་བཀག་པར། །སྣང་བ་གར་བདེ་ལྷུག་པར་བཞག
།དེ་ནས་རིག་པ་ཅུང་ཞིག་དངས།

།ཚོགས་དྲུག་ཡུལ་གྱི་སྣང་བ་འདི། །སླད་ཆེན་ཆང་གིས་མྱོས་པ་བཞིན།
།བྱུན་ནེ་ལོང་ངེ་ཟིངས་སེ་འདུག

།དུ་ཁ་ཐམས་ཅད་བདེ་བར་ཤར། །ནད་དང་གདོན་གྱི་རྟོག་པ་བྲལ།
།བླ་མ་སངས་རྒྱས་དངོས་སུ་མཐོང་། །ཉམས་ཉིད་འཛིན་ཆེན་པོར་ལམ་གྱིས་སློངས།
།བར་ཆད་མེད་པའི་ཇེང་ཅིག་ཐོབ། །གང་ལ་ལྟས་ཀྱང་སྙིང་རྗེ་སྐྱེ།
།དཔྱིད་ཀའི་ལྷུང་པོ་ལས་ཕཞོལ་འདྲ། །ཁམས་འདུས་པ་བར་པའི་འཆར་ལུགས་ལགས།

།རི་ཁྲོད་དབེན་པའི་ས་ཕྱོགས་སུ། །སྒྲུབ་པ་ཉམས་སུ་ལེན་དུས་སུ།
།སྐན་གྲུགས་བསོད་ནམས་བྱུང་བའི་ཚེ། །བར་ཆད་བདུད་དུ་ངོ་ཤེས་ཟིན།
།སྙིང་ཡང་མི་དགའ་ཚོད་ཀྱིས་སོང་། །ནོར་དང་ཉམས་ལེན་རྗེས་པ་ཡི།
།འདི་ལ་དགོས་པ་མི་འདུག་པས། །ལོ་ལམ་ཟླ་ཡིས་བཅད་དམ་མནོས།

།དེ་ནས་ནང་པར་ཕྱིན་པ་དང་། །ཉིན་རེ་འཕགས་ཀྱིན་ཉམས་རེ་དགའ།
།ལ་རེ་རྒྱལ་གྱིན་བློ་རེ་བདེ།

In that time and circumstance
    there was no one to ask about discomforts.
Faults occurred, but I had no remedies for impediments;
good qualities occurred, but I had no enhancements.

Reversing the attention inward
    I clearly remembered the oral instructions of the master.
Without blocking the conduct of natural expression
    I relaxed and let appearances be as they might.
Then intrinsic awareness somewhat cleared.

This appearance of the objects of the six groups,
as for an elephant crazed with beer,
was seething, shimmering, turbulent.

All suffering dawned as pleasure,
there was freedom from thoughts of illness and demons,
the master was actually seen to be a buddha,
experiences were taken on the path as great meditative
    concentration,
a confidence of freedom from obstacles was gained,
and wherever I looked compassion arose.
Like the reduced action of the spring wind,
the middle gathering of the constituents dawned.

While practicing meditation
    at a hermitage in an isolated place,
fame and offerings came.
Recognizing the obstacle as Māra
    I became deeply troubled.
I had no need for this trade of wealth for experience,
and wondered whether it would take years or months
    to eliminate.

Then in the morning I left,
every day going higher, feeling more content,
more at ease with every pass crossed.

།ཇི་ལྟར་བསམས་ཀྱང་དགེ་སྦྱོར་དང་། །ཚེ་ཞིང་གདུང་བ་རྒྱབ་ཏུ་བསྐྱུར།

།འདྲིས་རྗེས་མེད་པའི་ས་ཕྱོགས་སུ། །སྤྲང་པོའི་དམན་ས་གཟུང་བྱས་ཏེ།
།དགེ་སྦྱོར་གྱི་འདོམ་པ་ཚད་དུ་སྐྱོལ། །གཞན་ཚོས་སྐྱིད་གྱིས་སྡུག་ཉོར་མཐོང་།
།རང་ཉི་མ་འཛོམ་ཅ་ན་བདེ། །དབང་མེད་བསེ་རུས་འཁམས་སོས་འདུ།
།ཁམས་འདུས་པ་ཐ་མའི་འཆར་ལུགས་ལགས།

།ཡར་སྤྲང་པོ་བདག་རང་ཅིག་པུར་བསྒོམ་པ་ལས། །མཐོ་མཛེ་དང་སྐྱོ་བ་མན་ཆད་ནས།
།དམའ་རྒྱི་ལམ་འཁྲུག་པ་ཡན་ཆད་ལ། །ཡར་མ་བྱུང་པ་ལ་རྣམ་པ་མེད།

།ཕ་མཚན་ལྡན་གྱི་བླ་མ་ཡུན་དུ་བསྟེན། །ཆོས་སྟན་རྒྱུད་གྱི་གདམས་པ་མང་དུ་ཞུས།

།རང་ཅིག་པུར་བསྒོམས་པའི་ཡོན་ཏན་གྱིས། །དེ་ཐམས་ཅད་གྲོགས་སུ་འགྲོ་བར་བྱུང་།།

Bozer Pass

Whatever I thought applied to virtuous actions,
love and affection forsaken.

In an unfamiliar place
  I assumed the humble role of a beggar
    and took my vow of virtuous actions to the limit.
Others saw me buy suffering with happiness,
while I was comfortable without accumulations.
Soothing like a gentle breeze,
the final gathering of the constituents dawned.

Generally, when meditating alone as a beggar,
from leprosy and madness at the most
  down to disturbed dreams at the least,
there wasn't a thing that didn't happen.

Long I relied on the authentic master, my spiritual father.
I requested for Dharma many oral instructions of the aural
  transmission.

As a good quality of my solitary meditation,
they all became helpful.

Iti

༣

།།གླང་འཁོར་དུ་བཞེས་པ།།

།།ན་མོ་གུ་རུ།།

སྙིང་ནས་ཆོས་བཞིན་མཛད་པ་རྣམས། །ནོར་ནི་ཤིང་ཁའི་བྲེ་རྒྱུང་འདྲ།
།ཆགས་པ་མེད་པར་སྦྱིན་པ་ཐོང་།

།དལ་འབྱོར་གྱི་སྙིང་པོ་བླང་བའི་ཕྱིར། །མིག་འབྲས་བཞིན་དུ་ཚུལ་ཁྲིམས་སྲུངས།

།ངན་སོང་གི་རྒྱུ་བ་ཞེ་སྡང་ཡིན། །སྡིག་ལ་བབ་ཀྱང་བཟོད་པ་བསྒོམས།

།ལེ་ལོས་བདག་གཞན་དོན་མི་འགྲུབ། །དགེ་བའི་ལས་ལ་བརྩོན་པར་གྱིས།

།འཁྲུལ་པའི་བློ་ལ་ཐུན་མེད་ཀྱིས། །རྩེ་གཅིག་གི་དོན་ལ་ཉམས་སུ་ལོང་།

།བཙལ་བས་སངས་རྒྱས་མི་རྙེད་ཀྱིས། །རང་གི་སེམས་ཀྱི་མཚན་ཉིད་ལྟོས།

།ལར་དད་པ་དང་པོ་སོས་ཀའི་ན་བུན་འདྲ། །ཡལ་བའི་འཚམས་སུ་སྙིང་རུས་འཚོལ་ལོ།།

ཨིཐི

3

Sung at Langkor:

Namo Guru

For those who act from the heart according to Dharma,
wealth is like little birds in the top of a tree.
Give generously without attachment.

To extract the essence of the freedoms and endowments,
guard moral discipline like it's your eyeballs.

The root of the lower realms is hatred.
Cultivate patience though it means your life.

Your own aims and those of others aren't achieved with laziness.
Be diligent in virtuous actions.

There's no time for confused thoughts.
Practice the meaning of single-mindedness.

Buddha isn't found by searching.
Look at the characteristic of your mind.

Generally, faith is like spring mist at first.
Be brave at the vanishing point.

Iti

༨

།།ན་མོ་གུ་རུ།།

བླ་མ་རིན་པོ་ཆེ་ལ་ཕྱིས་ནས་བྱོན་ནས་གྲུམ་རིངས་ན་མདག་ཀ་མཛད་པའི་དུས་སུ་ལྕམ་མོ་ཅིག་སློ་རྩར་བྱོན་ནས། ལ་ལ་སྙིང་ཅན་ཡིན་ཟེར། ལ་ལ་སྨྱོན་པ་ཡིན་ཟེར། ལ་ལ་སྤྲུག་ཡོལ་ཡིན་ཟེར། ལ་ལ་ལས་འཕྲོ་ཅན་ཡིན་ཟེར། དེད་ཀྱི་རྣ་བས་དལ་བ་མ་སྨྱོང་ཟེར་ནས། ཡོ་རྒྱུས་མང་པོ་སྨྲད་དུ་བྱུང་བ་ལ། བླ་མས་མགུར་བཞེས་པ།།

།།ཁོ་བོ་སྙིང་པོ་དགེ་ཆཞེས་པས། །མི་ལ་ལ་སྙིང་ཅན་སྙིང་ཅན་ཟེར།
།སྤྲིང་བདག་རང་དང་སྙིང་མས་ཁྲེར་རམ་མཉོས།

།ཆགས་སྡང་གི་རྒྱལ་པོ་ཕ་ཡུལ་སྤྲངས། །ཞེན་པའི་རྒྱལ་པོ་ཟས་ནོར་སྤྲངས།
།གཟུང་འཛིན་གྱི་རྒྱལ་པོ་ཉེ་འབྲེལ་སྤྲངས། །ད་ལྟ་རྒྱལ་ཁམས་ཕྱོགས་མེད་བསྐོར།

།མི་ཆོས་ཀྱི་ཟླ་རུ་མ་འདོད་པས། །གར་སྡོད་གནས་སུ་ཤེས་ཙམ་ན།
།ཕ་ཡུལ་ཀུན་ཅི་དགའ་མ་དགའ་མཛོད།

།ཚོག་ཤེས་ནང་ནས་ཤར་ཙམ་ན། །ཟས་ནོར་ཀུན་སུ་དགའ་མ་དགའ་མཛོད།

།འགྲོ་དྲུག་ཕ་མར་ཤེས་ཙམ་ན། །ཉེ་འབྲེལ་ཀུན་སུ་དགའ་མ་དགའ་མཛོད།

།སྤྲིང་ད་རུང་སྙིང་མས་བྲེ་ཁྲེར་མཆི།

།མི་ལ་ལ་སྨྱོན་པ་སྨྱོན་པ་ཟེར། །སྤྲིང་བདག་རང་དང་སྨྱོ་ནས་འདུག་གམ་མཉོས།

།ཕོ་གདོན་དུ་བླ་མའི་གདམ་ངག་གཉོད། །མོ་གདོན་དུ་མཁའ་འགྲོས་བྱིན་གྱིས་བརླབས།

4

Namo Guru

When the precious lord left Labchi and was performing a sealed retreat at Gyamring, a lady came to the door and said, "Some say you're a fraud. Some say you're insane. Some say you're a ghost. Some say you're a bearer of residual karma. My ears are never at rest." There were many stories, so the master sang a song:

Since I'm beggar and spiritual friend,
some people say, "He's a fraud—a fraud!"
I wonder whether this beggar has been carried away by fraud.

I renounced a home, the king of attachment and hatred,
renounced food and wealth, the kings of craving,
and renounced relatives, the kings of grasping and fixation.
Now I aimlessly roam the land.

I don't want a companion in the secular life.
When wherever you stay is understood as a holy place,
do what you want with all these homes!

When contentment dawns from within,
do what you want with all this food and wealth!

When the living beings of the six realms
  are recognized as your parents,
do what you want with all these relatives!

So now the beggar's even more taken by fraud.

Some people say, "He's insane—insane!"
I wonder whether this beggar has gone insane.

In place of demons, I'm afflicted by the master's oral instructions;
in place of demonesses, I'm blessed by ḍākinīs.

།རྒྱབ་རྟེན་ཕྱག་རྒྱ་ཆེན་པོས་བགྲིས། །སྙིང་རླུང་དུ་རྟོགས་པ་འགྱུར་མེད་འབྱུང་།
།བློ་རྒོད་དུ་མི་རྟག་པ་རྒྱུད་ལ་སྐྱེས།

།རྫས་སྦྱོར་དང་དྲག་སྔགས་ཀྱིས་མི་ཐུལ་ཏེ། མི་ཚོས་ཀྱི་ཟླ་རུ་མི་འདོད་པས།

།སྤྲང་དུ་རུང་སྨྱོ་ཚབས་ཇེ་ཆེ་འགྲོ།

།མི་ལ་ལ་སྲོག་ཡོལ་སྲོག་ཡོལ་ཟེར། །སྤྲང་བདག་རང་དང་སྲོག་ཡོལ་བྲོ་འཆམ་མཉོས།

།གཞི་དུག་ལྔ་སྐྱེས་པའི་ཕ་ཡུལ་ན། །ཡོ་འབག་བསྟུད་པས་དགེ་སྦྱོར་ལྡེངས།

།ཆགས་སྡང་གི་དམག་ཚོགས་འཐུག་ལུགས་སམ། །རྣམ་རྟོག་གི་མདའ་ཆར་འབབ་ལུགས་སམ།
།ཉོན་མོངས་ཀྱི་མཚོན་རྩེ་རྣོ་ལུགས་སམ། །གཉེན་པོའི་ཟྲུ་ཀུ་ཞན་ལུགས་སམ།

།བདག་ཐར་པའི་སྲོག་རྩ་བཅད་ཀྱིས་དོགས། །བྱང་ཕོག་ཀུན་དགའ་ར་བ་རུ།
།འཁོར་འདས་གཉིས་ཀྱི་མདུན་མ་བསྒོགས། །སྐྱིད་སྡུག་གཉིས་ཀྱི་འདམ་ཀ་བྱུང་།

།ཉན་ངོ་ཤེས་པའི་གྲོས་ཅིག་འདུག།

།གཞི་དད་པ་བརྟན་པོའི་རྟ་ལ་ཞོན། །བརྩོན་འགྲུས་དྲག་པོའི་ལྕག་གིས་དྲབས།
།ཤེས་རབ་ཆེན་པོས་ཁ་ལོ་བསྒྱུར། འགྲོག་ལ་ཕྱིས་ཀྱི་གནས་ལ་གྲོས་ནས་ཕྱིན།

The Great Seal supports me from behind;
immutable realization arises in place of depression;
impermanence arises in my mindstream in place of agitation.

This isn't cured by remedies and violent mantras,
and I don't want a companion in the secular life.

So now this beggar becomes even more insane.

Some people say, "He's a ghost—a ghost!"
I wonder whether this beggar acts ghostly.

When I lived for several years
    in a home that was the ground
        from which the five poisons are born,
virtuous conduct was shaky.

Is that how the militant hordes of attachment and hatred
    concentrate?
Is that how the rain of the arrows of thought falls?
Is that how the points of the weapons of afflicting emotion
    are sharpened?
Is that how the lancet of the antidote is dulled?

Frightened of severing the artery of liberation,
    in the pleasant temple of the body I accumulated
        the requisites of both saṃsāra and nirvāṇa,
and have the choice of either happiness or suffering.

Listen to this advice about recognition:

Mounted on the steed of firm faith as a basis,
I struck with the whip of intense diligence.
A great transcendent knowledge took control,
and I fled to the glacier of Drok Labchi.

།བསམ་གཏན་གྱི་མཁར་པེ་མཐོན་པོ་ལ། །ཉིང་འཛིན་གྱི་སྒྲོ་མོ་འགྲིག་མོ་བཙུག།
།ཡིད་ཆེས་ཀྱི་སྒྲོ་བདན་ཆེན་པོས་མནན།

།རིག་པ་དངོས་མེད་ཀྱི་རང་གསལ་འདི། །སྐྱེ་མེད་ཀྱི་བརྟན་ས་འཛིན་འཛིན་འདྲ།

།སྤྲང་དྲ་རུང་སྒྲོག་ཡོལ་ཧེ་ཆེར་མཆི།

།མི་ལ་ལ་ལས་ཅན་ལས་ཅན་ཟེར། །བདག་རང་དང་ལས་འཕྲོ་དང་ལྡན་ནམ་མནོས།

།བདག་གིས་མ་བསྡད་སྔ་ནམ་གྱི་ཕྱོགས་སུ་འབྲུམ་དུ་ཕྱིན།
།དྲིན་ཅན་གྱི་བླ་མ་དང་མཇལ་ལགས་པས། །བུ་གཅིག་པ་ལམ་དུ་འཛུད་པ་བཞིན།
།ལམ་ནོར་དོགས་མཛད་གྱིན་ཐུགས་བརྩེ་བས་བསྐྱངས།

།ཕྱག་རྒྱ་ཆེན་པོའི་དོན་བསྟན་པས། །གདམ་ངག་ཆུ་ལ་ཆུ་བཞག་འདྲ།
།རྡོ་རྗེ་འཆང་ཆེན་བྱོན་ལགས་ཀྱང་། །དོན་དྲི་རྒྱུ་མེད་པར་བློ་ཐག་ཆོད།

།སྤྲང་དྲ་རུང་ལས་འཕྲོ་དང་ཧེ་ལྡན་མཆི།།

Chubar Region

At the high castle turret of mental stability,
the door of meditative concentration is shut
    and locked with the great bolt of confidence.

This insubstantial, naturally radiant, intrinsic awareness
    keeps clinging to its birthless stronghold.

So now this beggar's even more ghostly.

Some people say, "He's got the karma—the karma!"
I wonder whether I'm endowed with residual karma.

I didn't stay but wandered off in the direction of Nyanam.
When I met the kind master
    he led me on the path like an only son.
Concerned that the path could be mistaken,
he cared for me with a loving heart.

When he presented the meaning of the Great Seal,
the oral instructions were like water poured into water.
Even if great Vajradhara came,
I'd surely have nothing to ask about the meaning.

So now the beggar's endowed with even more residual karma.

Iti

༥

།ཀླང་འཁོར་དུ།།

ན་མོ་གུ་རུ།།

ང་ནམ་མཁའ་ལྷ་བུའི་རྣལ་འབྱོར་པ། །མཚན་ཉིད་སུས་ཀྱང་མི་རྟོགས་ཀྱིས།
།ཡོག་ལྷ་མ་སྐྱེ་སྐལ་མེད་ཀུན།

།ང་ཉི་ཟླ་ལྷ་བུའི་རྣལ་འབྱོར་པ། །ཀུན་ལ་སྙོམས་པ་ཤུགས་ལ་ཤར།
།ང་ལ་ཐུང་ཅིག་རིགས་ཅན་རྣམས།

།ང་ས་གཞི་ལྷ་བུའི་རྣལ་འབྱོར་པ། །འབྲས་བུ་གོང་དུ་སྤྱེལ་ནུས་ཀྱིས།
།ང་ལ་ཕུལ་དང་ལས་ཅན་རྣམས།

།ང་མདོ་རྒྱུད་ལྷ་བུའི་རྣལ་འབྱོར་པ། །ཚིག་རེས་ཤེས་རྒྱུད་གྲོལ་ནུས་ཀྱིས།
།ང་ལ་ཉོན་ཅིག་བློ་ལྡན་ཀུན།

།ང་གསེར་འགྱུར་ལྷ་བུའི་རྣལ་འབྱོར་པ། །ཡོན་ཏན་གཞན་ལ་བགོད་ནུས་ཀྱིས།
།ཡུན་དུ་སྟེན་ཅིག་ལས་ཅན་ཀུན།

།ང་ནོར་བུ་ལྷ་བུའི་རྣལ་འབྱོར་པ། །གསོལ་བ་བཏབ་ན་དགོས་འདོད་འབྱུང་།
།མོས་གུས་གྱིས་ཅིག་དད་པ་ཅན།

།ང་སེང་གེ་ལྷ་བུའི་རྣལ་འབྱོར་པ། །གཅིག་པུར་བསྡད་པས་རྩལ་གསུམ་རྫོགས།
།རི་ལ་སྡོད་ཅིག་སྙིང་རུས་ཅན།

།ང་ཕ་མ་ལྷ་བུའི་རྣལ་འབྱོར་པ། །བྱམས་པ་ཆེན་པོ་རྒྱུད་ལ་ཤར།
།རེ་ཚད་སྐྱིད་ཅིག་དམན་པ་ཀུན།

5

At Langkor:

Namo Guru

A yogi like the sky,
my characteristics are realized by none.
All you unfortunate ones—don't let perverse views arise!

A yogi like the sun and moon,
I naturally shine equally on all.
You of good spiritual race—drink from me!

A yogi like the earth,
I'm able to increase the fruit.
You with the karma—offer to me!

A yogi like sūtra and tantra,
I'm able to liberate a mindstream with each word.
All you intelligent ones—listen to me!

A yogi like gold tincture,
I'm able to establish good qualities in others.
All you with the karma—rely on me for a while!

A yogi like a wish-fulfilling gem,
I fulfill needs and desires if supplicated.
You faithful ones—have devotion!

A yogi like a lion,
I perfect the three dynamic states while living alone.
You brave ones—live in the mountains!

A yogi like a father and mother,
great love has dawned in my mindstream.
All you humble ones—raise your hopes!

།ང་བུ་ཆུང་ལྷ་བུའི་རྣལ་འབྱོར་པ། །ཆགས་པ་མེད་པར་སྤྱོར་ནུས་ཀྱིས།
།ང་ལ་སློངས་ཅིག་དབུལ་པོ་ཀུན།

།ང་རྒྱལ་པོ་ལྷ་བུའི་རྣལ་འབྱོར་པ། །ཅོག་གེ་བསྡད་པས་ལས་རྣམས་ཟིན།
།ཀུན་གྱི་སྤྱི་བོར་ཁུར་བས་བདེ།

།ང་བསེ་རུ་ལྷ་བུའི་རྣལ་འབྱོར་པ། །གཞན་གྱི་གྲོགས་ལ་མ་རྟེན་པར།
།རང་རིག་གྲོགས་དང་འགྲོགས་པས་བདེ།

།ང་པད་མ་ལྷ་བུའི་རྣལ་འབྱོར་པ། །ཡུལ་ལ་ཆགས་སྡང་མི་སྐྱེ་བས།
།ཚོགས་ན་འདུག་ཀྱང་ཤིན་དུ་བདེ།

།ང་རྒོད་པོ་ལྷ་བུའི་རྣལ་འབྱོར་པ། །ཆོས་ཉིད་ཀྱི་ནམ་ཕངས་མཐོན་པོ་ནས།
།འཁོར་འདས་གཉིས་མེད་དུ་མཐོང་བས་བདེ།

།ང་རྒྱ་མཚོ་ལྷ་བུའི་རྣལ་འབྱོར་པ། །སྣ་ཚོགས་མཚན་མ་ཅིར་སྣང་ཡང་།
།ཐམས་ཅད་ཆོས་ཉིད་དུ་རོ་ཅིག་བདེ།

།ང་རི་བོ་ལྷ་བུའི་རྣལ་འབྱོར་པ། །རྐྱེན་གྱིས་ཁ་དོག་ཐ་དད་ཀྱང་།
།དོན་འགྱུར་བ་མེད་པའི་རྣལ་འབྱོར་བདེ།

།ང་རལ་གྲི་ལྷ་བུའི་རྣལ་འབྱོར་པ། །རྣམ་རྟོག་གར་བྱུང་ཐད་ཀར་གཅོད།
།ཐུག་ཕྲད་ལམ་དུ་སློངས་པས་བདེ།

།ང་རྡོ་རྗེ་ལྷ་བུའི་རྣལ་འབྱོར་པ། །འཇིག་འབྲལ་མེད་པའི་དོན་རྟོགས་པས།
སྐུ་གསུམ་རང་ལ་ཤར་བས་བདེ།

A yogi like an infant,
I'm able to give without attachment.
All you poor ones—beg from me!

A yogi like a king,
I uphold activities while seated,
happy to be honored on the heads of all.

A yogi like a rhinoceros,
I don't depend on other companions,
happy to associate with the companion of intrinsic self-awareness.

A yogi like a lotus,
attachment and aversion to objects doesn't arise for me,
extremely happy even staying in a group.

A yogi like a vulture,
from high in the sky of the true nature,
I'm happy seeing the nonduality of saṃsāra and nirvāṇa.

A yogi like the sea,
whatever various characteristics appear,
I'm happy with the single taste of everything in the true nature.

A yogi like a mountain,
I have different hues due to circumstance,
but am happy with the yoga of immutable truth.

A yogi like a sword,
I sever instantly whatever thoughts arise,
happy to take the encounter as the path.

A yogi like a vajra,
I've realized the indestructible, inseparable truth,
happy that the three buddha bodies dawn in myself.

།ང་གླང་ཆེན་ལྟ་བུའི་རྣལ་འབྱོར་པ། །ཐབས་ཤེས་ཀྱི་མཐུ་སྟོབས་ནང་ནས་རྒྱས།
།གཞན་སྣང་ཟིལ་གྱིས་གནོན་པས་བདེ།

།ཕ་མཉམ་མེད་བླ་མའི་བཀའ་དྲིན་གྱིས། །ལུས་ཇི་ལྟར་བྱས་དང་དལ་བའི་ངང་།
།སེམས་ཇི་ལྟར་བྱས་དང་བདེ་བའི་ཀློ།

།ཆོས་ཐམས་ཅད་སེམས་སུ་མ་ཤེས་ན། །བརྗོད་བྱ་ལ་བསམ་གྱིས་མི་ཁྱབ་པས།
།ཚིག་གི་མཐའ་ལ་ཐུག་མེད་ཀྱིས།

།སྙིང་པོའི་དོན་ལ་གོམས་འདྲིས་གྱིས།།

A yogi like an elephant,
the force of method and transcendent knowledge grows
from within;
I'm happy overcoming the perceptions of others.

By the kindness of the peerless spiritual father and master,
whatever the body does is a state of leisure,
whatever the mind does is a state of contentment.

If all phenomena aren't understood to be mind,
even with all these inconceivable expressions,
the end of words will never be reached.

Get used to the essential meaning.

Iti

༦

ན་མོ་གུ་རུ།།

ཀོ་བོས་རྩྭི་རི་ཁྲུར་སྐར་དུ་བསྒོམས་པའི་ལོ་ལ། རྩི་རི་བྱང་ན་སེང་གེ་རྫོང་ན་མཆེད་པོ་ཧོ་སྲུས་པད་ཞེ་བཞུགས་པ་ལ་མཇལ་དུ་ཕྱིན་པས། ཁོང་ན་རེ་འུ་མཇལ་བ་དགའ་བོ་གསུངས་ནས། ཉིད་རྣལ་འབྱོར་པ་རབ་ཏུ་བྱུང་བ་ཡིན་ན་དབྱངས་འདྲ་མེད་དམ། དབྱངས་ཅིག་མཛོད་དང་གསུང་། དབྱངས་ཀུན་དང་ང་བཀྲེང་ནས་མི་ཇ་བྱས་པས། མི་སྐྱོ་ཡིས་རི་ཁྲོད་འདི་རུ་དི་རིང་དབྱངས་ཅིག་མཛོད་གསུང་ནས། དེའི་དུས་སུ་འདི་གླངས་སོ།།

།ཕ་བླ་མ་རྣམས་ལ་ཕྱག་འཚལ་ལོ། །བཀའ་དྲིན་ཅན་ལ་སྐྱབས་སུ་མཆི།

།ལ་སྟོད་རྒྱལ་གྱི་རྩི་རི་འདི། །གྲུབ་ཐོབ་གོང་མའི་བཞུགས་སར་བརྟའ།
།མཁའ་འགྲོ་འདུ་བའི་གནས་ཆེན་དུ། །དགེ་སློང་གླུ་ལེན་མི་འོས་ཏེ།
།མཆེད་པོ་གོང་མའི་བཀའ་མི་བཅག། །གླངས་ཀྱང་བཀའ་སློལ་བཟང་བར་བརྟའ།

།བསྟོད་པ་གླུ་རུ་ལེན་པ་དེ། །ཤཱཀྱ་ཐུབ་པའི་བཀའ་སློལ་ལགས།
།མིང་ཡང་འཇམ་དཔལ་མཚན་བརྗོད་ཟེར།

།དེ་ནས་མཐོང་སྣང་གླུ་རུ་ལེན་པ་དེ། །སྲས་བྱང་ཆུབ་སེམས་དཔའི་བཀའ་སློལ་ལགས།
།མིང་ཡང་བདེར་གཤེགས་མཚན་བསྟོད་ཟེར།

།དེ་ནས་མཆོད་པ་གླུ་རུ་ལེན་པ་དེ། །འཁོར་ཉན་ཐོས་ཆེན་པོའི་བཀའ་སློལ་ལགས།
།མིང་ཡང་འབྱོར་པའི་ཐུས་གསུམ་ཟེར།

།རྟོགས་པ་གླུ་རུ་ལེན་པ་དེ། །བྲམ་ཟེ་ཆེན་པོའི་བཀའ་སློལ་ལགས།
།མིང་ཡང་མདོ་ཧ་སྐོར་གསུམ་ཟེར།

6

Namo Guru

During the year I was meditating at Kyurgar on Mt. Tsi, I went to meet brother Josey Payshey who was living at Senge Dzong north of Mt. Tsi. He said, "I'm happy to meet you." Then he exclaimed, "If you're an ordained yogi, don't you have some songs? Sing a song!"

I replied, "No, a song in front of everyone would embarrass me."

"No problem," he said. "Sing a song in this hermitage today!"

I sang this at that time:

Homage to the masters, my spiritual fathers;
I take refuge in your kindness.

This Mt. Tsi of the Victors in Ladö
  is the residence of former adepts.
In a great holy site where ḍākinīs gather,
it isn't right for a monk to sing songs.
But I won't defy the order of a respected brother,
and there is a fine tradition of singing.

The singing of praise in song
  was the tradition of Śākyamuni,
known by name as *The Recitation of the Names of Mañjuśrī.*

Then the singing of visions in song
  was the tradition of his spiritual sons, the bodhisattvas,
known by name as *The Praise of the Names of the Sugata.*

Then the singing of offerings in song
  was the tradition of his retinue, the great śrāvakas,
known by name as *The Three Things of Wealth.*

The singing of realization in song
  was the tradition of the Great Brahmin,
known by name as *The Dohā Trilogy.*

།ཉམས་མྱོང་སླུ་རྟུ་ལེན་པ་དེ། གྲུབ་ཐོབ་གོང་མའི་བཀའ་སྲོལ་ལགས།
།མིང་ཡང་ཉམས་ཀྱི་སྐྱི་རྩུལ་ཟེར།

།གོ་ཚོད་སླུ་རྟུ་ལེན་པ་དེ། །བདག་གིས་དི་རིང་བཀའ་སྲོལ་གཟུང་།
།མིང་ཡང་སྒོམ་པའི་ཉམས་དབྱངས་ཟེར།

།བདག་དམ་པ་ཆོས་ཀྱི་སྒོར་ཞུགས་ནས། །ཕ་མཚན་ལྡན་གྱི་བླ་མ་རིན་ཆེན་ལ།
།ཚིག་དོན་གཉིས་ཀྱི་སྒྲོ་འདོགས་བཅད། །ཡིདས་བ་མེད་པར་ཉམས་སུ་བླངས།
།རྒྱུན་ཆད་མེད་པའི་གོ་བ་སྐྱེས།

།ཕྱི་ཚོགས་དྲུག་ཡུལ་ལ་ཕར་བལྟས་པས། །སེམས་སྐྱེ་མེད་ཚོ་འཕྲུལ་ཡིན་པར་མཐོང་།

།ནང་རིག་པ་སེམས་ལ་ཚུར་ལྟས་པས། །གཞི་རྩ་བྲལ་གྱི་སེམས་ཉིད་ཡེ་ནས་སྟོང་།

།བར་དྭན་རིག་བློ་ལ་བརྟགས་བྱས་པས། །བློ་བུར་གྱི་རྟོག་པ་རང་སར་གྲོལ།

།དེ་ལྟར་ནང་དུ་གོ་བ་འདི། །ཕྱག་རྒྱ་ཆེན་པོའི་ལྟ་བ་ཡིན།

།འདི་དུམ་བུ་རྒྱུན་དུ་བསྐྱིངས་པ་ཡིས། །རྫེ་རྡོ་རྗེ་འཆང་གྲོན་ལགས་ཀྱང་།
།བྲི་རྟུ་མེད་པར་བློ་ཐག་ཆོད།

།དེ་ལྟར་གོ་བའི་སྤྲང་པོ་བདག །རྣལ་འབྱོར་རབ་ཏུ་བྱུང་བ་འདི།
།ལྟ་བ་དམན་པ་མ་ལགས་ཏེ། །སྒོམ་པ་གསུམ་ལྡན་བྱེད་པ་ལགས།

The singing of experience in song
 was the tradition of former adepts,
known by name as the way experience is born.

The singing of understanding in song
 is the tradition upheld by me today,
known by name as the experiential song of meditation.

After I entered the gate of the excellent Dharma,
with the precious, authentic master as spiritual father,
doubts of both word and meaning were removed.

Practicing without distraction,
a ceaseless understanding was born.

Looking out at the external objects of the six groups,
I saw them to be the magical display of birthless mind.

Looking in at the internal, intrinsic awareness of mind,
there was the groundless, rootless nature of mind that is
 forever empty.

Examining the attentive, aware mind in between,
incidental thoughts free themselves.

An inner understanding such as this
 is the view of the Great Seal.

The Tumbu man continually sustaining this
 is sure he'd have nothing to ask
  even if great lord Vajradhara came.

As a beggar that's how I understand it.
This being an ordained yogi isn't a low viewpoint,
it's acting with the three vows.

།ཆོས་གོས་སྣོད་གསུམ་ཆཞམས་པ་འདི། །སྲིད་པ་ཆེ་བ་མ་ལགས་ཏེ།
།སངས་རྒྱས་ཀྱིས་གསུངས་པའི་གོས་གསུམ་ལགས།

།ཁྲིམས་ཉིས་བརྒྱ་ལྔ་བཅུ་སྲུང་བ་འདི། །རྣམ་རྟོག་ཆེ་བ་མ་ལགས་ཏེ།
།ལས་རྒྱུ་འབྲས་ལ་ཡིད་ཆེས་སྐྱེས་པ་ལགས།

།ཅིག་ཕུར་དབེན་པར་བསྡོད་པ་འདི། །མི་ཆོས་སྐྱོང་པ་མ་ལགས་ཏེ།
།སེམས་སྐྱེ་མེད་ཉམས་སུ་ལེན་པ་ལགས།

།ཞལ་ལྷ་བ་རྣམས་ཀྱི་ཐུགས་དགོས་དེ་ལ་མཛོད།།

This arrangement of three lower Dharma robes
  isn't from great attachment,
it's the three robes prescribed by the Buddha.

This preservation of two hundred and fifty rules
  isn't just a lot of ideas,
it's born of a belief in the causes and results of actions.

This living alone in solitude
  isn't a snub at secular life,
it's the practice of birthless mind.

There's your advice;
be happy and act upon it.

Iti

༥

།།ན་མོ་གུ་རུ།།

ཡང་ཁོ་བོས་མཁན་པ་ཁྲིད་དུ་མདག་ཆར་ལ་སྤྱད་པའི་དུས་སུ། །མཆེད་པོ་གཉིས་ལོག་པ་མཐོང་ནས།
།དེའི་དུས་སུ་འདི་སྐད་ཅེས་སྨྲས་སོ།

།དད་པ་སྐྱེ་བ་སླ་བར་ཛ་སྟེ། །སྐྱེ་ཤིས་འཛིགས་པ་དཀའ་བར་ཛ།

།ཆོས་སྒྲོར་འཇུག་པ་སླ་བར་བཛ་སྟེ། །འཁོར་བས་སྐྱོ་བ་དཀའ་བར་བཛ།

།དགོན་པ་སྟེན་པ་སླ་བར་བཛའ་སྟེ། །བྱ་བ་ཐོངས་པ་དཀའ་བར་བཛ།

།བླ་མ་སྟེན་པ་སླ་བར་བཛའ་སྟེ། །ཡོན་ཏན་ལོངས་པ་དཀའ་བར་བཛ།

།ཟབ་དོན་ཐོས་པ་སླ་བར་བཛ་སྟེ། །རྒྱུད་ལ་སྐྱེ་བ་དཀའ་བར་བཛ།

།སེམས་བསྐྱེད་བགྲི་བ་བསླ་བར་བཛའ་སྟེ། །གཞན་དོན་ནུས་པ་དཀའ་བར་བཛ།

།དབང་རྣམས་ཐོབ་པ་སླ་བར་བཛ་སྟེ། །དམ་ཚིག་ཐུབ་པ་དཀའ་བར་བཛའ།

།ཆོས་སྒྲོར་འཇུག་པ་སླ་བར་བཛའ་སྟེ། །མི་ཆོས་ཚོལ་བ་དཀའ་བར་བཛའ།

།ཆོས་ཟབ་དགུ་བཤད་པ་སླ་བར་བཛ་སྟེ། །རང་རེ་ཐོག་ན་གནས་པ་དཀའ་བར་བཛ།

།ཆོས་མཐོན་པོ་སྨྲ་བ་སླ་བར་བཛའ་སྟེ། །དོན་རྒྱུད་ལ་ཐེབས་པ་དཀའ་བར་བཛའ།

7

Namo Guru

Once, when I was staying in sealed retreat at the Khenpa charnel ground, I saw two brothers give up. This is what I said at that time:

> The birth of faith is easy;
> destruction by birth and death is hard.
>
> Entering the Dharma circle is easy;
> weariness with saṃsāra is hard.
>
> Relying on solitude is easy;
> giving up things to do is hard.
>
> Relying on a master is easy;
> adopting good qualities is hard.
>
> Hearing the profound truth is easy;
> birth in the mindstream is hard.
>
> Awakening the enlightenment mind is easy;
> the ability to benefit others is hard.
>
> Receiving initiations is easy;
> keeping the sacred commitments is hard.
>
> Entering the Dharma circle is easy;
> fending off secular life is hard.
>
> Explaining many profound Dharmas is easy;
> living them yourself is hard.
>
> Talking about high Dharma is easy;
> applying the meaning to the mindstream is hard.

།སྣང་བ་འགྱུར་བ་སླུ་བར་བརྡའ་སྟེ། །མཐའ་རུ་ཐོན་པ་དཀའ་བར་བརྡའ།

།མེད་པའི་ཞིག་པོ་སླུ་བར་བརྡ་སྟེ། །ཡོད་ལ་ཆགས་མེད་དཀའ་བར་བརྡའ།

།ལར་འདི་འདྲ་བཤད་ན་ཟད་པ་མེད།

ཅེས་སྨྲས་སོ།།

ཨིཐི

Transforming appearances is easy;
keeping it to the end is hard.

Destruction of the nonexistent is easy;
no attachment to the existent is hard.

Generally, explanation like this is endless.

So I said.

Iti

༨

།།གླང་འཁོར་དུ།།

ན་མོ་གུ་རུ།

ཡང་ཁོ་བོའི་ལུས་ལ་ནད་ཤིན་དུ་ལྕི་བ་ཅིག་བྱུང་སྟེ། མི་ན་བ་རྣ་བའི་རྩེ་མོ་གཉིས་ལས་མེད་དེ། འཚམས་བཅད་ནས་བསྙེན་པ་བཏོང་གིན་ཡོད་པ་ལ། ཉིན་ཅིག་ཕ་རོལ་དུ་ཕྱིན་པའི་ཆོས་ལ་ལྟ་རྟོག་བྱས་ནས་བསྒོམས་པས། །ནང་དུ་འདི་ལྟར་གོ་སྟེ། ད་ནི་ན་བ་འདིས་མཆོད་ནས་འདུག། འདི་མིན་ན་མི་ཚེ་ཏབ་ཏེབ་ལ་མཛད་པར་འདུག། འདིས་ཆོས་མིན་ན་མི་ནུས་པར་འདུག་པས། །འདི་ལོ་བཅུ་མ་དྲག་ན་ཡིད་དམ་གྱི་ཞལ་མཐོང་ཟིན། །འདི་མ་དྲག་ན་དགའ་བར་འདུག་སྙམ་པ་བཅོས་མ་མ་ཡིན་པ་ཅིག། རྒྱུད་ལ་སྐྱེས་པས་སེམས་ཀྱང་བདེ་འཁོལ་སོང་ནས། ད་སྟིང་པོ་བསྒྲངས་ན་སངས་དྲག་པ་སྲིད་པས། །ཕྲེང་བ་ཡང་རྩིག་ལོགས་ལ་བཀལ་ནས་ཉལ་བས། སྟོན་ནས་གཉིད་ཆག་པ་དང་། སེམས་ལ་བདེ་བ་སྐྱེད་པ་དེས་གཉིད་དུ་ཁྲིགས་སོང་སྟེ། གཉིད་སད་པ་དང་ནམ་ཕྱེད་དུ་སོང་ནས་འདུག་པས་ལུས་ཀྱི་ན་བ་ཅིག་དང་མི་འདུག་སྟེ། བདེན་ནམ་བརྫུན་སྙམ་ནས། ལངས་པས་ལྡང་ཤེས་པར་བྱུང་། ལར་ཆོས་ཉིད་ཡིན་པར་འདུག་སྟེ། གང་ཟག་གིས་མ་བྱུང་བར་འདུག་སྙམ་ནས། དེའི་དུས་སུ་འདི་སྐད་ཅེས་སྨྲས་སོ།

།ཕ་བླ་མ་རྣམས་ལ་ཕྱག་འཚལ་ལོ། །ཡིད་དམ་ལྷ་ཡི་དངོས་གྲུབ་སྩོལ།

།གཞི་གཏིང་ནས་དད་པ་སྐྱེས་པ་དང་གཅིག། །དམ་པའི་ཆོས་སྒྲོར་ཞུགས་པ་དང་གཉིས།
།མི་ཆོས་རྒྱབ་ཏུ་བསྐྱུར་བ་དང་གསུམ།

།ཆོས་འདི་གསུམ་བཏོག་ན་རྣལ་འབྱོར་པ་ལགས་ཏེ། །ཁྲིད་ཆོས་མེན་སྤྱོད་ལ་དཀན་ཏེར་མཆིའོ།

།བླ་མའི་དྲིན་གྱིས་ཟིན་པ་དང་གཅིག། །ཕ་ཡུལ་རྒྱབ་ཏུ་བསྐྱུར་བ་དང་གཉིས།
།རི་ཁྲོད་དགོན་པ་འགྲིམ་པ་དང་གསུམ།

8

At Langkor:

Namo Guru

Once, an oppressive disease appeared on my body. Only the two tips of my ears were not afflicted. I went into retreat and practiced the propitiation. One day I meditated after consulting the teachings on the Perfections. This is how I understood it within.

The unfabricated thought arose in my mindstream, "Now I'm tormented by this disease. Without this, a human lifetime would be carelessly wasted. Because of this, I can't do anything except Dharma, so if I'm not cured of this in ten years, I'll have already seen the face of the chosen deity. I'd rather not be cured of this."

My mind became content and relaxed. Now, since a cure was possible if I recited the heart mantra, I hung the beads on the wall and slept. My sleep was disrupted before, but now because I had found peace of mind, I fell asleep. When I awoke it was the middle of the night. There was no disease on my body. "Is this true or false?" I wondered. I arose and could stand. I thought, "In general, this is due to the true nature of phenomena; it doesn't happen because of the individual."

At that time I said this:

Homage to the masters, my spiritual fathers.
Grant the attainment of the divine chosen deity.

First is deeply born faith as the ground.
Second is entering the gate of the excellent Dharma.
Third is forsaking the secular life.

If you have these three qualities, you're a yogi.
It's impossible for you to act against Dharma.

First is being held by the master's kindness.
Second is forsaking a home.
Third is wandering in isolated mountain ranges.

།ཆོས་འདི་གསུམ་བདོག་ན་རྣལ་འབྱོར་པ་ལགས་ཏེ། །ཁྱོད་ཕ་ཡུལ་དུ་བསྡད་པ་དཀའ་ཏེར་མཆིའོ།

།ཕྱི་ཐོས་པས་ཚིག་ཏུ་ཟིན་པ་དང་གཅིག །ནང་བསམས་པས་དོན་གོ་བ་དང་གཉིས།
།དོན་སྒོམས་པས་ཉམས་སུ་མྱོང་བ་དང་གསུམ།

།ཆོས་འདི་གསུམ་བདོག་ན་རྣལ་འབྱོར་པ་ལགས་ཏེ། །མྱོངས་པ་ཁྱེད་ལ་དཀའ་ཏེར་མཆིའོ།

།ལུས་སྐྱེད་རིམས་ཀྱིས་ལྷ་སྐུར་གསལ་བ་དང་གཅིག །རླུང་རྫོགས་རིམས་ཀྱིས་སྟོང་པར་ཤེས་པ་དང་
གཉིས། །སེམས་འོད་གསལ་འགྱུ་འོང་མེད་པ་དང་གསུམ།

།ཆོས་འདི་གསུམ་བདོག་ན་རྣལ་འབྱོར་པ་ལགས་ཏེ། །ཁྱོད་ཐ་མལ་དུ་སྡོད་ལ་དཀའ་ཏེ་མཆིའོ།

།ཕྱི་འཁོར་བ་ལ་སྐྱོ་བ་སྐྱེས་པ་དང་གཅིག །ནང་མི་རྟག་པས་བློ་སྣ་བསྡུ་པ་དང་གཉིས།
།བྱམས་སྙིང་རྗེ་རྒྱུད་ལ་སྐྱེས་པ་དང་གསུམ།

།ཆོས་འདི་གསུམ་བདོག་ན་རྣལ་འབྱོར་པ་ལགས་ཏེ། །ཁྱེད་རང་དོན་སྒྲུབ་པ་ལ་དཀའ་ཏེར་མཆིའོ།

།ནད་དགེ་སྦྱོར་གྱི་སྐུལ་མར་ཤེས་པ་དང་གཅིག །བགེགས་ཡིད་དམ་གྱི་ལྷ་རུ་ཤེས་པ་དང་གཉིས།
།རིག་པ་ན་འཁན་རྡོ་ཡིས་ཟིན་པ་དང་གསུམ།

།ཆོས་འདི་གསུམ་བདོག་ན་རྣལ་འབྱོར་པ་ལགས་ཏེ། །ཁྱེད་སྤྱངས་འཕྲོ་མེད་ལ་དཀའ་ཏེར་མཆིའོ།

།ཞེས་གླུ་རུ་བླངས་སོ།།

ཨོཾཐ

If you have these three qualities, you're a yogi.
It's impossible for you to stay in a home.

First is external apprehension of the words through listening.
Second is internal understanding through contemplation.
Third is experiencing the meaning through meditation.

If you have these three qualities, you're a yogi.
It's impossible for you to be ignorant.

First is the body radiant as the divine buddha body
through the creation stage.
Second is understanding it as empty
through the perfection stage of the vital winds.
Third is no fluctuation in the radiant light of the mind.

If you have these three qualities, you're a yogi.
It's impossible for you to remain ordinary.

First is the birth of weariness with saṃsāra.
Second is reining in the mind with impermanence.
Third is the birth of love and compassion in the mindstream.

If you have these three qualities, you're a yogi.
It's impossible to practice for your own benefit.

First is knowing an illness to be an admonition to virtuous action.
Second is knowing an impediment
to be the divine chosen deity.
Third is the patient's recognition of intrinsic awareness.

If you have these three qualities, you're a yogi.
It's impossible for you to have nothing left to practice.

So I sang in song.

Iti

༩

།།ན་མོ་གུ་རུ།

ཀོ་བོ་ཤཱཀྱའི་དགེ་སློང་ལྷོམ་བུ་བས། །མཚོ་མ་ཕམ་གི་བྱང་ནུབ། །གད་པ་གསེར་གྱི་བྱ་སྐྱིབས་ལ་སྟ་ལོའི་ལོ་མ་ཟ་ཡིན་བསྡད་ནས། །ནུབ་ཅིག་བསམས་པས་སྣང་རྩལ་སྦྱར་དང་མི་འདྲ་བ་ཅིག་བྱུང་ནས་གླངས་པ།

།ཕྱི་ཚོགས་དྲུག་ཡུལ་གྱི་སྣང་བ་འདི། །མ་རྟོགས་པའི་དུས་ན་འཁྲུལ་སྣང་ལགས།
།ཆགས་སྡང་རྨོངས་གསུམ་སྐྱེད་པར་བྱེད།

།རྟོགས་པའི་དུས་ན་ཆོས་སྐུ་ལགས། །ཡེ་ཤེས་ཀྱི་རྩལ་སྣང་རྒྱས་པར་བྱེད།

།དོན་མཐར་ཐུག་ལ་སྣང་མེད་ཞེན་པ་མེད།

།བློ་ཁ་ནང་དུ་བལྟས་པའི་རིག་པ་འདི། །མ་རྟོགས་པའི་དུས་ན་སེམས་ཅན་ལགས།
།གནས་འགྲོ་བ་དྲུག་ཏུ་འཁོར་བར་བྱེད།

།རྟོགས་པའི་དུས་ན་སངས་རྒྱས་ལགས། །སྐུ་གསུམ་རང་ལས་འཆར་བར་བྱེད།

།དོན་མཐར་ཐུག་ལ་འཁོར་འདས་གཉིས་སུ་མེད།

།རི་ཁའི་བྲག་ཕུག་སྟོང་པ་འདི། །མ་རྟོགས་པའི་དུས་ན་འདྲེ་ཅན་ལགས།
།འཇིགས་ཤིང་ཡ་ང་སྐྱེད་པར་བྱེད།

།རྟོགས་པའི་དུས་ན་གཞལ་ཡས་ཁང་། །ཉམས་བྲོད་པར་ཅན་རྒྱུད་ལ་བསྐྱེད་པར་བྱེད།

།དོན་མཐར་ཐུག་ལ་གང་ན་འདུག་ཀྱང་བདེ།

།འཁྲུལ་སྣང་གདོན་བགེགས་ཀྱི་ཆོ་འཕྲུལ་འདི། །མ་རྟོགས་པའི་དུས་ན་ལྷ་འདྲེར་བཟ།

9

Namo Guru

When I was staying as a mendicant Buddhist monk eating knotweed leaves at Gepa Sergyi Chagyib northwest of Lake Mapham, one night my thoughts appeared in a different way than before, and I sang:

When there's no realization, these external appearances
of the objects of the six groups are confusing appearances.
Desire, hatred, and ignorance are produced.

When there is realization, they're the buddha body of reality.
The dynamic appearances of primordial awareness expand.

In the ultimate sense there are no appearances and no attachment.

When there's no realization, this intrinsic awareness observed
when the mind is turned inward is a sentient being.
It circles through the realms of the six living beings.

When there is realization, it's a buddha.
The three buddha bodies dawn in ourselves.

In the ultimate sense saṃsāra and nirvāṇa are not two.

When there's no realization, this empty stone cave
on the mountain face is haunted.
Fear and terror are produced.

When there is realization, it's a celestial palace.
An exceptional experience is produced in the mindstream.

In the ultimate sense anywhere is pleasant.

When there's no realization, these confusing appearances and
apparitions of demonic impediment are gods and ghosts.

།བར་ཆད་དང་ཐོ་འཚམ་རྩོལ་བར་བྱེད།

།རྟོགས་པའི་དུས་ན་ཡིད་དམ་ལྷ། །མཆོག་དང་ཐུན་མོང་དངོས་གྲུབ་སྟེར།

།དོན་མཐར་ཐུག་ལ་ལྷ་འདྲེ་བས་བདག་ཀྱང་མེད།

།ལུས་འབྱུང་བཞིས་བསྡུས་པའི་གཡར་པོ་འདི། །མ་རྟོགས་པའི་དུས་ན་བརྫོས་བཅས་ལགས།
།ནད་དང་དུ་ཁ་སྐྱེད་པར་བྱེད།

།རྟོགས་པའི་དུས་ན་རྒྱལ་བའི་སྐུ། །མཚན་དང་དཔེ་བྱད་མཐོང་སྣང་ཙམ།

།དོན་མཐར་ཐུག་ལ་སྒྱུ་མའི་དཔེ་བྱད་འདྲ།

།ཡར་བདག་ལ་དགའ་བའི་ཉམས་ཅིག་ཤར།།

ཨི་ཐི

Obstacles and abuse are energetically created.

When there is realization, they're the divine chosen deity.
The sublime and common attainments are given.

In the ultimate sense the self is more nonexistent than
the gods and ghosts.

When there's no realization, this loan of a body comprised
  of the four elements is tangible.
Illness and suffering are produced.

When there is realization, it's the buddha body of the Victor.
It's just a visual appearance with the marks and characteristics.

In the ultimate sense it's like the characteristics of an illusion.

In general, a joyful experience dawned for me.

Iti

༡༠

།།ན་མོ་གུ་རུ

ཡང་ཕོ་བོས་ལ་ཕྱིས་གདངས་ཀྱི་ར་བ་རྟ། སེང་གེ་བྲག་ལ་བསྒོམས་པའི་དུས་སུ། ཉིན་གཅིག་རྨི་ལམ་ན་རང་དང་མཆེད་པོ་དགེ་སློང་ཡིད་བཞིན་གཉིས་ཤི་ནས། རྒྱལ་པོ་ཅིག་གི་བུ་མོ་སྤུན་གཉིས་སུ་སྐྱེས་ནས་འདུག་པས། །ཕོ་ན་རེ་འུ་གཉིས་བུད་མེད་འདྲའི་སྐྱེ་བ་དམན་པ་ཟེར་བ་ལ། །མི་ཕོ་བོས་ཡབ་རྒྱལ་པོ་འདི་འདྲ་བའི་སྲས་མོར་ནི་སྐྱེས། དམ་པའི་ཆོས་ནི་བྱུར་ཡོད། བྱང་ཆུབ་ཀྱི་སེམས་ལ་ཕོ་མོ་མེད་ཀྱིས། དེ་བས་བདག་གི་དབྱངས་འདི་ལ་ཉོན་དང་བྱས་ནས། དེའི་དུས་སུ་རྨི་ལམ་དུ་བླངས་པ།

ཧྲི་བླ་མ་འདི་དམུ་ལོང་གི་མིག་སྤྱུ་དང་འདྲ། །རང་དད་གུས་མོས་པས་གསོལ་བ་འདེབས་ནུས་ན།
།མ་ནོར་ཐར་པའི་ལམ་སྣ་འདྲེན་པར་ངེས་ཀྱིས།

།མོས་གུས་ཀྱིས་ཅིག་དད་པ་ཅན་ཀུན།

།བླ་མའི་གདམ་ངག་འདི་བདུད་རྩི་དང་འདྲ། །དོན་ཉམས་སུ་མྱོང་བར་འཐུང་ནུས་ན།
།ནང་དུག་ལྔའི་གཙོང་ནད་ཞི་བར་ངེས་ཀྱིས།

།རང་ངེས་ཤེས་སྐྱེད་ཅིག་དད་པ་ཅན་ཚོ།

།ཆོས་ལྟ་བ་འདི་བྱ་རྒྱལ་གྱི་རྒོད་པོ་དང་འདྲ། །ཐབས་ཤེས་རབ་ཀྱི་གཤོག་རྩ་མ་ཆག་ན།
།དོན་ཆོས་ཉིད་ཀྱི་དགུང་དང་མཇལ་བར་ངེས་ཀྱིས།

།ཟུང་འཇུག་ལམ་དུ་སློང་ཅིག་དད་པ་ཅན་ཚོ།

།དོན་སྒོམ་པ་འདི་ཁྲི་གདུགས་ཀྱི་ཉི་མ་དང་འདྲ། །རྒྱུད་རྣམ་རྟོག་གི་སྤྲིན་གྱིས་མ་གཡོགས་ན།
་ ་ོ་ ་ ་ོ་ ་ ་ི་ ་ ་ ་ ་བར་ངེས་ཀྱིས།

10

Namo Guru

Once, I was meditating at Senge Drak in the glacial enclosure of Labchi. One day, in a dream, both I and a brother, the monk Yizhin, had died and been reborn as two sisters who were the daughters of a king. Yizhin said, "The two of us have low births as women," but I replied, "We've been born as daughters with a king such as this for a father. We have the excellent Dharma to practice. There's no male and female enlightenment mind! So listen to this song of mine." At that point I sang in the dream:

> This lord and master is like a guide for the blind.
> If we're able to pray with faith and devotion,
> he'll surely lead us on the infallible path to liberation.
>
> All you faithful ones—have devotion!
>
> This oral instruction of the master is like nectar.
> If we're able to drink the meaning through experience,
> the chronic illness of the five poisons within will surely be cured.
>
> You faithful ones—produce certainty yourselves!
>
> This Dharma view is like the vulture, king of birds.
> If the wings of method and transcendent knowledge
> aren't broken,
> the space of the true nature of reality will surely be encountered.
>
> You faithful ones—take total integration as the path!
>
> This meditation on reality is like the brilliant sun.
> If the mindstream isn't veiled by clouds of thought,
> the obscurations of the afflicting emotions will surely be
> incinerated.

།རིག་པ་དངས་ · · · · · ·ཅིག་དད་པ་ཅན་ཚོ།

།ལམ་སྦྱོད་པ་འདི་གི་ལིང་གི་ཡན་པ་དང་འདྲ། །སེམས་ཆགས་སྡང་གི་སྒྲོག་ཏུ་མ་བཅུག་ན།
།སྟོང་ཉིད་བདེ་ཆེན་གྱི་ཐང་ལ་རྒྱུག་པར་ངེས་ཀྱིས།

།གཉིས་འཛིན་སྦྱོངས་ཅིག་དད་པ་ཅན་ཚོ།

།འབྲས་བུ་འདི་ཡིད་བཞིན་གྱི་ནོར་བུ་དང་འདྲ། །ཉམས་ལེན་ཞེན་རྩེ་ཅིག་གྱི་དོར་བྱེད་ནུས་ན།
།གཞན་དོན་ལྷུན་གྲུབ་ཏུ་འབྱུང་བར་ངེས་གྱིས།

།དོན་ཉམས་སུ་ལོང་ཅིག་དད་པ་ཅན་ཚོ།

།ཆོས་དམ་ཚིག་འདི་ཤེལ་དཀར་གྱི་སྒྲུམ་ཐུང་དང་འདྲ། །རང་སེམས་དག་པས་འཛིན་ནུས་ན།
།དངོས་གྲུབ་ཀྱི་ཁང་ཐོག་ཏུ་ཕྱིན་པར་ངེས་ཀྱིས།

།རང་སེམས་དྲང་པོར་སྲོང་ཅིག་དད་པ་ཅན་ཚོ།

།འདྲ་བ་བདུན་གྱི་དབྱངས་ཆུང་འདི། །ལ་ཕྱིས་གངས་ཀྱི་ར་བ་རུ།
།རྨི་ལམ་གྱི་བར་དོར་གླངས་པ་ལགས།

།དབྱངས་འདི་ལ་མཁའ་འགྲོའི་བྱིན་བརླབས་བདོག་གོ།

ཨི་ཐི

You faithful ones—keep intrinsic awareness clear!

This conduct of the path is like the freedom of a fine horse.
If the mind isn't put in the chains of desire and hatred,
it will surely race upon the plain of emptiness and great bliss.

You faithful ones—reject clinging to duality!

This result is like a wish-fulfilling gem.
If we're able to cleanse it with single-minded practice,
the benefit of others will surely occur spontaneously.

You faithful ones—practice the meaning!

This sacred commitment of Dharma is like a small crystal ladder.
If we're able to scale it with the purity of mind itself,
we'll surely arrive on the rooftop of the house of attainments.

You faithful ones—keep mind itself straight!

This little song of seven likenesses
  was sung in the intermediate state of dream
    in the glacial enclosure of Labchi.

This song has the blessing of the ḍākinīs.

Iti

༡༡

།།ན་མོ་གུ་རུ

།ཡོན་ཏན་རིན་པོ་ཆེ་འབྱུང་བའི་གནས། །སྟོན་པའི་དམ་ཆོས་དར་བའི་ས། །རིག་པ་ཞེས་པ་དངས་པའི་ཡུལ། བཀྲ་ཤིས་ཁ་དམར་གྱི་དགོན་པ་རུ། །སྣང་བ་མི་བདེན་པར་གོ། །འཁོར་བས་སྐྱོ་བར་གོ་ནས། །ཐང་སྐྱ་དང་ དྲིལ་བུ་ཡང་སྦྱིན་ནམ་སྙམ་པའི་དུས་སུ། །གླུ་འདི་གླངས་སོ།

།རྗེ་བཀའ་དྲིན་ཅན་ལ་སྐྱབས་སུ་མཆི།

།བདག་དམ་པ་ཆོས་ཀྱི་སྒོར་ཞུགས་ནས། །ཚེ་འདིའི་ཆེ་ཐབས་མ་བསྒྲུབས་པར།
།བློ་སེམས་ཕྱི་མའི་ཕྱོགས་སུ་བཏང་།

།ལྷང་ཚད་ཆུང་ཡང་བདག་མི་འགྱོད།

།མཚན་ལྡན་གྱི་བླ་མ་སྟེན་དུས་སུ། ལོག་ལྟའི་མཉམ་འགྲོགས་མ་བགྱིས་པར།
།མཉེས་པ་གསུམ་གྱིས་མཆོད་པ་ཕུལ།

།དགུང་དུ་གཤེགས་དང་བདག་མི་འགྱོད།

།འདུས་བྱས་མི་རྟག་མཚན་ཉིད་གོ། །དལ་འབྱོར་ཤུལ་རིངས་དལ་བར་མཐོང་།
།འཁར་ལན་བྱེད་སྙིང་མ་འཚལ་བས།

།ཁང་ཁྱིམ་ངན་དང་བདག་མི་འགྱོད།

།འགྲོ་དྲུག་དྲིན་ཅན་ཕ་མར་མཐོང་། །ཐོབ་པའི་ལོངས་སྤྱོད་བཀྲེ་ནས་བཏང་།
།མ་ཐོབ་པ་ལ་འདོད་པ་མེད།

11

Namo Guru

At the monastery of Tashi Khangmar, the source of precious good qualities, the site of the spread of the excellent Dharma of the Teacher, and the place where intrinsic awareness and cognition cleared, I understood that appearances are untrue, and I understood the deceptions of saṃsāra. When I was wondering whether to give away even my painted image and bell, I sang this song.

I take refuge in the kind lord.

After entering the door of the excellent Dharma,
without accomplishing the prideful ambitions of this life,
I turned my attention toward the next.

I have few assets, but I've no regrets.

When relying on the authentic master,
I presented the offering of the three delights
  without associating with perverted view.

He's departed into space, but I've no regrets.

Impermanence was understood to be the characteristic
  of composite things.
The long road to the freedoms and endowments
  was seen to be exhausting.

With no heart for building work, my residence may be poor,
but I've no regrets.

The six kinds of living beings were seen to be our kind parents.
The wealth I'd received was distributed and given away.
I've no desire for what I haven't received.

།འཛོམ་ཤེས་ཆུང་ཡང་བདག་མི་འགྱོད།

།སྙིགས་མའི་ཚེ་ལ་སྐྱིད་ཞེན་མེད། །ཡུན་དུ་བསྡད་ཡོང་མེད་མཐོང་ནས།
།ཚིག་བཞག་དོན་ལ་ཉམས་སུ་བླངས།

།ད་ལྟ་ཤི་ཡང་བདག་མི་འགྱོད།

།ཤཱ་ཀྱའི་བསྟན་ལ་རབ་བྱུང་ནས། །བསོད་སྙོམས་ཀྱིས་འཚོ་བར་ཁས་བླངས་ནས།
།འཕྲུལ་བྱུང་འཕྲུལ་དག་དམ་བཅའ་བདོག

།འཚོ་རྒྱུགས་ཆད་དང་བདག་མི་འགྱོད།

།ནད་དང་དུ་ཁའི་མུན་གསེབ་ཏུ། །ཐར་པའི་འགྲོ་ལམ་སྟོར་པ་ལ།
།གགས་སེལ་གྱི་ཉི་མས་ལམ་སྣ་དྲངས།

།རང་དོན་ལུས་དང་བདག་མི་འགྱོད།

།སྨོན་ལམ་གྱིས་འབྲེལ་པའི་བུ་སློབ་ལ། །མཐོན་དམན་ཉེ་རིང་མ་བགྱིས་པར།
།ཟབ་མོའི་གདམས་པ་རྩད་ནས་བྱིན།

།ཆོས་བཞིན་མི་བྱེད་ཀྱང་བདག་མི་འགྱོད།

།སྤུགས་ཕྱི་མ་གཉིས་ཀྱི་ཡི་དམ་ལ། །སྒྲོ་གསུམ་ཐ་མལ་དུ་མ་བཞེན་པར།
།འབྲལ་བ་མེད་པར་བཟླས་བརྗོད་བྱས།

།བྱིན་བརླབས་ཆུང་ཡང་བདག་མི་འགྱོད།

Little has been accumulated, but I've no regrets.

In degenerate times there's no serenity.
Seeing there's no time to stay long,
I put aside the words and practiced the meaning.

I could die now and have no regrets.

Taking ordination in the Śākya Doctrine,
I agreed to live by begging alms,
and have the vow to live on what appears
from moment to moment.

Supplies may run out, but I've no regrets.

In the darkness of illness and suffering
I lost the path leading to liberation,
but was guided on the path by the sun
of the removal of impediments.

Self-interest was lost, but I've no regrets.

For disciples connected by prayers,
without regard for high and low, or close and distant,
I completely gave the profound oral instructions.

They may not practice according to Dharma, but I've no regrets.

For the chosen deities of the final two sets of mantra,
I constantly performed the recitations,
without clinging to body, speech, and mind as ordinary.

The blessing may be small, but I've no regrets.

།ཇི་ཙམ་གྱི་ཟས་ནོར་གཉིས་ལ་ལོངས་སྤྱོད་ཀྱང་། །གཞན་དོན་དུ་བསྔོས་པ་མ་རྟོགས་པ།

།རང་དོན་དུ་བཟུང་པ་ཁབ་ཙིག་མེད།

།བསོག་འཇོག་བྱུང་ཡང་བདག་མི་འགྱོད།།

ཨྠི།།

Whatever has been enjoyed of both food and wealth
has been dedicated for the benefit of others,
without a single needle kept for my own benefit.

Accumulation may occur, but I've no regrets.

Iti

༡༣

།འདི་ཡང་ཁང་མར་དུ།།

ན་མོ་གུ་རུ།།

ཡང་དེའི་རྗེས་མ་ཚེ་འདིའི་སྣང་བ་ལ་མངོན་པར་ཞེན་ཅིང་བཅགས་པ་རྣམས་བློ་སྣ་བསྒྱུར་བའི་ཕྱིར་འདི་བྲིས་སོ།

།ཕུང་པོའི་བདག་འཛིན་མ་སྤོངས་པས། །ཕོ་ཀའི་ལྷ་ལ་གསོལ་བཏབ་ཀྱང་།
།འཁོར་བའི་དུ་ཁ་མི་སྐྱོབས་ཀྱིས། ལྷ་དཀོན་མཆོག་གསུམ་ལ་མོས་གུས་གྱིས།

།ཐམས་ཅད་ཕ་མར་མ་ཤེས་ན། །དུད་གསུམ་དང་གཉེན་གཞི་བསྐྱངས་ལགས་ཀྱང་།
།ཆོས་དང་འཐུན་པར་མི་འགྱུར་གྱིས། །བླ་མ་དང་མཆེད་ལ་གུས་པར་གྱིས།

།རང་ཅིག་པུར་བདེ་བར་མ་ཤེས་ན། །མི་འཚོགས་མང་པོའི་གཡེང་བའི་རྒྱུ།
།འཁྲུལ་གཏམ་དང་ཉོན་མོངས་སེམས་ལ་གནོད། །དབེན་པའི་གནས་སུ་བག་ཡོད་སྤྱོད།

།ཚིག་ཤེས་ནང་ནས་མ་སྐྱེས་ན། །ཡོངས་སྤྱོད་དང་འདུ་འཛི་འཁོར་བའི་རྒྱུ།
།ཕྱུག་ཀྱང་རྟག་དུ་མི་སྤྱོད་ཀྱིས། །ཟང་ཟིང་གི་ནོར་ལ་ཞེན་པ་བསྐྱུངས།

།གནས་ལུགས་ལ་ངེས་ཤེས་མ་སྐྱེས་ན། །ཚིག་ཤེས་ཀྱིས་གཞན་དོན་འབད་བྱས་ཀྱང་།
།གློན་པོས་བླུན་པོ་མི་འགྲོངས་ཀྱིས། །སྙིང་པོའི་དོན་ལ་གོམ་འདྲིས་གྱིས།

།རྒྱུད་ཚོད་མཐོ་རུ་མ་སོང་ན། །ཚུལ་དང་སྤྱོད་པ་བཟང་བཙོས་ཀྱང་།

12

This was also at Khangmar:

Namo Guru

Once, after that, I wrote this to rein in the minds of those obsessed with and attached to the appearances of this life:

When clinging to a self among the aggregates hasn't been
  abandoned,
even though mundane deities are supplicated,
there will be no protection from the sufferings of saṃsāra.
Be devoted to the divine Three Jewels.

If all have not been recognized as our parents,
even though the three officials and four friends are guarded,
it won't be in accord with the Dharma.
Be devoted to the masters and brothers.

If happiness hasn't been recognized when alone,
a group of many people will be a cause of distraction.
Confused talk and afflicting emotions harm the mind.
Practice restraint in an isolated place.

If contentment hasn't arisen from within,
possessions and turmoil will be causes of saṃsāra.
Even though rich, don't always indulge.
Reduce attachment to material wealth.

If certainty about the way things really are hasn't arisen,
effort may be made to benefit others with knowledge of the words.
But fools shouldn't lead fools.
Get used to the essential meaning.

If the measure of the mindstream hasn't increased,
even though a fine style and conduct are adopted,

།བཟང་རྟགས་ཀྱི་ཡོན་ཏན་མི་འཆར་གྱིས། །དེ་བས་རང་རེའི་སྤྱོད་པ་གྱིས།

།དིང་སང་སྙིགས་མ་ལྔ་བདོའི་དུས། །མི་རྣམས་ལྷ་སྤྱོད་མི་མཐུན་པས།
།ཡ་ཁ་དང་སྒྲོ་སྐུར་མི་ཁྲེགས་ཀྱིས། །རང་གི་ཆོས་འཐུན་ལམ་དུ་ཁྲེར།

།སེམས་ཅན་གྱི་འདོད་པ་མ་ཟད་པས། །ཐམས་ཅད་མགུ་བར་མི་ནུས་གྱིས།
།ཕ་རོལ་གྱི་སྐྱོན་ལ་མ་རྟོག་པར། །དེ་བས་རང་རེ་སེམས་ཁྲལ་བསྐྱངས།

།ཚེ་འདིའི་སོག་ཆོས་མཁས་གྱུར་ཀྱང་། །སང་ནང་བར་འཆི་བའི་དུས་བྱུང་ན།
།ཆོས་མཁས་ལ་བསྡུད་དུ་མི་བདོག་གིས། །ད་ལྟ་རང་ནས་འཆི་ཆོས་མཛོད།

།འདོད་ཡོན་གྱི་མཚན་ཉིད་འཕྲུལ་དུ་བདེ། །སྤྱོད་ངེས་ཀྱི་རྣམ་སྨིན་ཕྱོག་ཏུ་གྱུར།
།སླུ་མེད་ཀྱི་བཀའ་ལ་ཡིད་ཆེས་གཞན། །ངན་སོང་རྟོག་སྣ་དྲེད་པར་མཆིའོ།

།བླ་མ་དང་དགོན་པ་མ་སྟེན་པར། །ཕ་ཡུལ་ལ་གཡག་ཆགས་བྱེད་པ་ཆོ། །
འཁྲུལ་པའི་ཉོན་མོངས་འདྲིས་པ་སླ། །བག་ཆགས་ངན་པས་གོས་པར་མཆིའོ།

།བདག་ལ་དད་ཅིང་གུས་པ་རྣམས། །དོན་དེ་ལེགས་པར་སེམས་ལ་ཞོག།

།རིན་པོ་ཆེའི་གསུང་། རྗེའི་ཞབས་ལ་འདུད།།

the good qualities of the signs of excellence won't dawn.
We must practice the conduct instead.

Today when fivefold degeneracy is rampant,
the views and conduct of people aren't in harmony.
Unhindered by mockery, exaggeration, or denigration,
take them on the path in harmony with our Dharma.

Since there's no end to the desires of sentient beings,
all cannot be pleased.
Not thinking about the faults of others,
we must reduce our own worries instead.

Even though skilled in the business affairs of this life,
if the moment of death comes tomorrow morning,
those skilled in business won't get to stay.
Practice the Dharma for death right now.

The characteristic of sensual gratification is immediate pleasure.
The maturation certain to be experienced is concealed.
Weak belief in an infallible teaching
  is the mental prelude to the lower realms.

Not having relied on a master and solitude,
for those who are attached to their yaks at home,
familiarity with confused afflicting emotion is easy
  while clothed in evil habitual propensities.

Those with faith and respect for me,
keep these points well in mind.

The speech of the precious one. I bow at the lord's feet.

Iti

༧༣

།།ན་མོ་གུ་རུ།།

བཀའ་རྒྱུད་རྩོད་པ་མེད་པར། །ཕྱོགས་མེད་ཡོངས་སུ་གྲགས་ནས།
།ཀུན་གྱི་སྤྱི་བོར་ཁུར་བའི་རྒྱུད་པ་འདི་ཉམས་རེ་དགའ།
།གྲུབ་ཐོབ་རྒྱུན་ཆད་མེད་པ་འདི་དང་རེ་སྤྲོ།

།མཚན་ཉིད་ཀུན་དང་འཐུན་པར། །དོན་གཉིས་ཕུན་སུམ་ཚོགས་ནས།
།ཡིད་བཞིན་ནོར་བུ་ལྟ་བུའི་བླ་མ་འདི་ཉམས་རེ་དགའ།
།དགོས་འདོད་ཐམས་ཅད་འབྱུང་བ་འདི་དང་རེ་སྤྲོ།

།མདོ་རྒྱུད་ཀུན་དང་འཐུན་པར། །སེམས་ཉིད་གཏན་ལ་ཕབ་ནས།
།སངས་རྒྱས་ལག་ཏུ་བཏོང་བའི་གདམས་ངག་འདི་ཉམས་རེ་དགའ།
།ངེས་ཤེས་འཕྲུལ་དུ་སྐྱེ་བ་འདི་དང་རེ་སྤྲོ།

།ཕ་ཡུལ་རྒྱབ་ཏུ་བསྐྱུར་ནས། །དམིགས་བརྟད་གཞི་གཟུང་མེད་པར།
།ཕྱོགས་མེད་རི་ཁྲོད་འགྲིམ་པའི་དགོན་པ་འདི་ཉམས་རེ་དགའ།
།འཁར་ལན་བསྲུང་རན་མི་དགོས་པ་དང་རེ་སྤྲོ།

།ཟོལ་ཟོག་གཡོ་སྒྱུ་སྤངས་ནས། །ངོ་བསྲུང་རྩོལ་བ་མེད་པར།
།གར་སྐྱིད་ལྷོམ་བུ་བྱེད་པའི་འཚོ་བ་འདི་ཉམས་རེ་དགའ།
།སེར་སྣས་སྡུག་སོགས་མི་དགོས་པ་དང་རེ་སྤྲོ།

།ཡོ་ག་བྲུ་བ་བཏང་སྟེ། །མི་ཆོས་རྒྱབ་ཏུ་བསྐྱུར་ནས།
།གྲོགས་མེད་ཅིག་པུར་སྡོད་པའི་སྒྲོམ་ཆེན་འདི་ཉམས་རེ་དགའ།
།སྣབས་ཆཤལ་བུ་ཚ་མི་དགོས་པ་དང་རེ་སྤྲོ།

13

Namo Guru

The indisputable Kagyu
  is famous everywhere.
This lineage that is honored on everyone's heads is so delightful.
This unbroken stream of adepts is so wonderful.

In accord with all the characteristics
  and the excellent two goals,
this master who is like a wish-fulfilling gem is so delightful.
This fulfillment of all needs and wishes is so wonderful.

In accord with all sūtra and tantra,
the nature of mind is established.
This oral instruction that places buddhahood
  in the hand is so delightful.
This immediate birth of certainty is so wonderful.

Forsaking a home
  and not holding to a basic point of reference,
this solitude of aimlessly wandering the mountain ranges
  is so delightful.
No need to protect a structure is so wonderful.

Abandoning deceit and guile,
and with no effort in face-saving,
this life of a mendicant who is happy anywhere is so delightful.
No need to suffer from greed and so forth is so wonderful.

Renouncing mundane activities
  and forsaking the secular life,
this meditator living alone without companion is so delightful.
No need for snotty, diarrhetic children is so wonderful.

།སེམས་ཀྱི་མཚན་ཉིད་རྟོགས་ནས། །ཐེ་ཚོམ་ཡིད་གཉིས་མེད་པར།
།དོན་ལ་ངེས་ཤེས་སྐྱེད་པའི་ལྟ་བ་འདི་ཉམས་རེ་དགའ།
།རང་ངོ་རང་གིས་ཤེས་པ་འདི་དང་རེ་སྲོ།

།འོད་གསལ་འགྲོ་འོང་མེད་པར། །འབྲལ་མེད་རྒྱུན་དུ་ཤར་ནས།
།རྣམ་རྟོག་ཆོས་སྐུར་ཤེས་པའི་སྒོམ་ཆེན་འདི་ཉམས་རེ་དགའ།
།ཐུན་མཚམས་སུ་རྒྱུན་ཆད་མེད་པ་དང་རེ་སྲོ།

།གཟའ་བརྟད་ཚུལ་འཆོས་མེད་པར། །བྱེད་མཁན་ངོ་ཡིས་ཟིན་ནས།
།སྣ་ཚོགས་ལམ་དུ་སློངས་པའི་སྤྱོད་པ་འདི་ཉམས་རེ་དགའ།
།ཅི་བྱེད་གྲོགས་སུ་འགྲོ་བ་འདི་དང་རེ་སྲོ།

།བྱས་ཆོས་ཕྱི་ནས་ཞིག་སྟེ། །བྱུང་ཆོས་ནང་ནས་ཤར་ནས།
།ཆོས་རྣམས་ཟད་སར་སྐྱོལ་བའི་འབྲས་བུ་འདི་ཉམས་རེ་དགའ།
།སྐུ་གསུམ་རང་ལ་ཤར་བ་འདི་དང་རེ་སྲོ།།

ཨེ་མ།

ཨིཐི

Realizing the characteristic of mind,
with no doubts and indecision,
this view producing certainty in the truth is so delightful.
This natural recognition of our essence is so wonderful.

Radiant light without fluctuation,
continually dawning without separation,
this meditator recognizing thoughts
  to be the buddha body of reality is so delightful.
No interruption between sessions is so wonderful.

Without point of reference and pretension,
the actor is recognized.
This conduct that takes the variety as the path is so delightful.
This state in which anything done becomes helpful is so wonderful.

Dharma that's done is destroyed from without.
Dharma that happens dawns from within.
This result that brings phenomena to the point of cessation
  is so delightful.
This dawning of the three buddha bodies in ourselves is so
  wonderful.

E Ma

Iti

༡༨

།།སྤྲ་མགྲོག་ཏུ། དགོན་པའི་བཀྲ་ཤིས་ལ་གཤེགས་པའི་དུས་སུ། སེ་མིག་པའི་ཉ་མ་སྐྱིལ་ཐུང་མ་ཆོས་ཞུས་ནས། བླ་མ་སེ་མིག་པའི་སྐྱུན་སྤུར་བཞེས་སོ།།

།།ན་མོ་ར་ཏྣ་གུ་རུ།

གཞོན་ནུ་ལང་མཚོ་འདི་སོས་ཀའི་མེ་ཏོག་དང་འདྲ། །མི་རྟག་ཡལ་བའི་ཆོས་ཀྱང་བསྟན།
།གཞོན་པ་ལྷ་ཆོས་བྱེད་པ་མེད། །དབྱངས་སླངས་པས་ཕན་པར་ཀྱང་མ་མཐོང་ངོ་།

།ལུས་རྒྱས་པ་རི་མཐོའི་གྲིབ་མ་དང་འདྲ། །ཧྲིང་ནས་ལྡོག་པའི་ཆོས་སྟན་ཀྱང་།
།རྒྱས་པ་འཆི་བ་དྲན་པ་མེད། །དབྱངས་སླངས་པས་ཕན་པར་ཀྱང་མ་མཐོང་ངོ་།

།རང་འཆི་བ་འདི་བྱ་འཕུར་གྱི་གྲིབ་མ་དང་འདྲ། །ཐོག་ཏུ་འབབ་པའི་ཆོས་སྟན་ཀྱང་།
།ཕྱི་མ་དོན་དུ་གཉེར་བའི་མི་ཡང་མེད། །དབྱངས་སླངས་པས་ཕན་པར་ཀྱང་མ་མཐོང་ངོ་།

།ལོངས་སྤྱོད་འདི་སྦྲང་མའི་སྦྲང་རྩི་དང་འདྲ། །རང་བོར་ནས་འགྲོ་བའི་ཆོས་བསྟན་ཀྱང་།
།ཟས་ཚོགས་སུ་གཏོང་བའི་མི་ཡང་མེད། །དབྱངས་སླངས་པས་ཕན་པར་ཀྱང་མ་མཐོང་ངོ་།

།གཉེན་ཉེ་འབྲེལ་འདི་ཚོང་འདུས་ཀྱི་འགྲོན་པོ་དང་འདྲ། །སྨྱུར་དུ་བྲལ་བའི་ཆོས་བསྟན་ཀྱང་།
།འབྲེལ་པ་གོང་དུ་གཅོད་པའི་མི་ཡང་མེད། །དབྱངས་སླངས་པས་ཕན་པར་ཀྱང་མ་མཐོང་ངོ་།

།ལར་དལ་འབྱོར་འདི་རྩ་ཁའི་ཟིལ་པ་དང་འདྲ། །སྡོད་ལོང་མེད་པའི་ཆོས་སྟན་ཀྱང་།

14

When he went to the auspicious rites for the monastery at Bagyog, Semikpa's female disciples who escorted him for a short distance made a request, and he sang in the presence of master Semikpa.

Namo Ratna Guru

This youthful vitality is like a flower in spring.
The Dharma of fading impermanence is taught,
but the young don't practice the divine Dharma,
and I haven't seen singing a song help.

The aging of the body is like the shadow of a high mountain.
The Dharma that it starts from the beginning is taught,
but the old aren't mindful of death,
and I haven't seen singing a song help.

This death of ours is like the shadow of a bird in flight.
The Dharma of a sudden descent is taught,
but no one is energetic toward the next life,
and I haven't seen singing a song help.

This wealth is like a honey bee's honey.
The Dharma of leaving it behind is taught,
but no one gives everything away to the assembly,
and I haven't seen singing a song help.

These friends and relatives are like visitors in a marketplace.
The Dharma of a rapid separation is taught,
but no one severs the connection in advance,
and I haven't seen singing a song help.

Generally, these freedoms and endowments are like dew
on a blade of grass.
The Dharma that they won't last long is taught,

།ཕྱོ་སྣ་སྟུང་བའི་མི་ཡང་མེད། །དབྱངས་གླངས་པས་ཕན་པར་གྱུར་མ་མཐོང་ངོ།

།ཅེས་པ་འདི་ལ་ཕྱིས་ནས་འཐོན་པའི་དུས་སུ་སྣ་ནང་པ་མཁྱོག་ན་དགོན་པའི་བཀྲ་ཤིས་ལ་ཡོན་བདག་པོ་མོ་མང་པོ་འཚོགས་པའི་དུས་སུ། བླ་མ་རིན་པོ་ཆེ་སེ་མིག་པའི་ཞལ་ནས་ལོད་གསུང་ནས་གླངས་སོ།།

Mt. Tseringma

but no one reins in the mind,
and I haven't seen singing a song help.

When I left Labchi, many male and female sponsors had gathered for the auspicious rites of the monastery at Bagyog in Nyanang. This was sung when the precious master Semikpa said, "Sing!"

༩༥

།།ཁོ་བོ་སྣང་འཁོར་མཆིས་ཀྱི་སྤྲང་པོ་འདི། །སྟོན་ཚོགས་དང་སྨོན་ལམ་གྱི་རྒྱུ་རྫོགས་པས།
།ད་ལྟ་མཚན་ལྡན་གྱི་རྗེ་དང་མཇལ། །གུས་པས་སངས་རྒྱས་དངོས་སུ་མཐོང་།

།ཐུགས་སེམས་དབྱེར་མེད་འདྲེས་པ་ནི། །གདམ་ངག་ཆུ་ལ་ཆུ་བཞག་འདྲ།

།ཕྱག་རྒྱ་ཆེན་པོའི་དོན་གོ་བས། །རྡོ་རྗེ་འཆང་ཆེན་བྱོན་ལགས་ཀྱང་།
།གཟུགས་སྐུ་སེམས་ཀྱི་རྣམ་འཕྲུལ་ཡིན། །དོན་དྲི་རྒྱུ་མེད་པར་བློ་ཐག་ཆོད།།

15

I'm this Langkor beggar
   who completed the causes of the assemblies
      and prayers before,
met an authentic lord now,
and through devotion saw him as a real buddha.

When mind and enlightened mind indivisibly blended,
the oral instructions were like water poured into water.

I understood the meaning of the Great Seal.
Even if great Vajradhara came,
the buddha body of form is just a mental emanation.
I'd surely have nothing to ask about the meaning.

༡༨

།བླ་མ་རིན་པོ་ཆེ་རྣམས་ལ་ཕྱག་འཚལ་ལོ།།

བདག་མཆིས་ཀྱི་རྣལ་འབྱོར་འདུག་པ་འདི། །བྱམས་སྙིང་རྗེ་གཉིས་ཀྱིས་རྒྱུད་སྦྱངས་ནས།
།བརྩེ་བའི་སེམས་ཀྱིས་ངོས་འདེབས་ཀྱིས། །གདུང་བའི་སེམས་ཀྱིས་ཉན་པར་ཞུ།

།དཀའ་བཅད་སྡོང་གི་ཐོབ་དཀའ་བའི། །རྨེ་ཟན་དང་འདྲའི་མི་ལུས་འདི།
།དོན་ཡོད་བགྲིས་ན་མི་རུང་ངམ།

།ཀྱེ་མ་སོམས་དང་དད་ལྡན་རྣམས། །མི་ལུས་ངོས་ལ་སྲན་ཆགས་འདྲ།
།འགྲོ་དྲུག་སེམས་ཅན་དྲངས་ལ་ལྟོས།

།རྒྱུ་འབྲས་འགྲོ་དྲུག་ས་བོན་འདྲ། །གང་བཏབ་སྨིན་པའི་ཚུལ་ལ་ལྟོས།

།ལ་ལ་སྡུག་བསྔལ་གྱི་རྒྱུ་ལ་སྤྱོད། །ལ་ལ་སྡུག་བསྔལ་གྱི་འབྲས་བུར་གནས།
།འཁོར་བ་འདི་ལ་སྙིང་མེད་ཀྱིས།

།བདེན་ཞེན་གྱི་དངོས་པོ་བློ་བཟློག་ལ། །མོས་གུས་རྒྱུན་ཆད་མེད་པ་ཡིས།
།སྐྱོ་ངས་མེད་པའི་བླ་མ་སྟེན།

།དད་པ་ཡལ་བ་མེད་པའི་ས། །ཀྱོ་ཤས་མེད་པར་གདམ་ངག་ཉོན།

།ཤེས་རབ་རྫོངས་པ་མེད་པ་ཡིས། །ཡེངས་པ་མེད་པར་བློས་སུ་ལོང༌།

16

Homage to the precious masters.

I'm this yogi whose mindstream
  has been refined with both love and compassion.
I give advice with kind intentions.
Please listen with a sympathetic mind.

Difficult to gain through a thousand hardships,
this human body is like a most precious object.
Wouldn't it be right to make meaningful use of it?

Alas! Think about it, faithful ones.
A human body is like a pea stuck to a wall.
Look at the number of sentient beings in the six realms.

Cause and result are like the seeds
  of the six kinds of living beings.
Watch how what is planted ripens.

Some engage in the causes of suffering;
some abide in the results of suffering.
There's no happiness in this saṃsāra.

Turn the mind away from things held to be true,
and with unceasing devotion
  rely on a master without sadness and fatigue.

With faith that doesn't fade,
listen to the oral instructions without weariness.

With unclouded discernment,
take them to mind without distraction.

།སྙིང་རུས་ལྷེམ་ཀྱུང་མེད་པ་ཡིས། །རྒྱུན་ཆད་མེད་པར་བྱང་ཆུབ་སྒྲུབས།

།རང་འདོད་མེད་པའི་ཕན་སེམས་ཀྱིས། །ཉེ་རིང་མེད་པར་གཞན་དོན་བྱེད།

།སྔ་ཕྱི་མེད་པའི་མཉམ་རྗེས་ཀྱིས། །དུས་རྣམས་རྟག་ཏུ་ཟིན་པར་མཛོད།

།ཕྱོགས་རིས་མེད་པའི་ལྟ་བ་ཡིས། །མཐའ་བྲལ་ཆེན་པོར་གོ་བར་མཛོད།

།མ་ཡེངས་རྒྱུན་གྱི་བསྒོམས་པ་ཡིས། །འབྲལ་བ་མེད་པར་ཉམས་སུ་ལོང་།

།གྲོགས་སུ་འགྲོ་བའི་སྤྱོད་པ་ཡིས། །བྱེད་མཁན་ངོ་ཡིས་ཟིན་པར་མཛོད།

།རང་ངོ་ཤེས་པའི་འབྲས་བུ་ཡིས། །ཆོས་རྣམས་ཟད་སར་སྐྱོལ་བར་མཛོད།

།ཟོལ་ཟོག་མེད་པའི་དམ་ཚིག་གིས། །ཁས་བླངས་མཐར་ཏུ་ཕྱིན་པར་མཛོད།།

ཨིཐི།།

With unshakable courage,
achieve enlightenment without interruption.

With unselfish, helpful intentions,
work for the benefit of others without prejudice.

Without absorption before and maintenance after,
uphold it all the time.

With an impartial view,
know the great boundless state.

With undistracted, continual meditation,
practice without interruption.

With conduct that contributes to this,
recognize the actor.

With the result of self-recognition,
bring phenomena to the point of cessation.

With undeceiving, sacred commitments,
keep the promises to the end.

Iti

༡༢

།།ཨོཾ་ས་སྟི།

བདག་རང་སྤྲང་པོ་རྣལ་འབྱོར་པ། །ཐོས་པས་ཕྱིའི་སྒྲོ་འདོགས་ཆོད།
།བསམས་པས་དེ་ཉིད་དོན་དུ་གོ། །བསྒོམས་པས་ཉམས་སུ་མྱོང་ལགས་པས།

།བག་ཆགས་ངན་པ་བསག་པའི་ཕ་ཡུལ་དུ། །ཡོ་འགའ་སྤྱད་པས་དགེ་སྦྱོར་ལྷེངས།

།གནས་རི་ཁྲོད་དགོན་པར་སྒོམ་དུ་ཕྱིན། །རང་སེམས་རྟོགས་པ་དང་ཏུག་གིས་མཇལ།

།ཡེངས་པ་མེད་པར་ཉམས་སུ་བླངས། །རྒྱུན་ཆད་མེད་པའི་གོ་བ་སྐྱེས།

།ད་ལྟ་སེམས་ལ་རག་ལས་མི་བདོག་པས། །སྐྱེ་མེད་ཐག་ཆོད་ཀྱི་སྟེང་ན་བློ་རེ་བདེ།

།བདག་ཡང་ན་རི་ཁྲོད་དགོན་པ་འགྲིམ། །ཡང་ན་ཕུག་ཏུ་འདག་ཆར་བྱེད།
།ཚོགས་གསེབ་ཏུ་འདུག་ན་རྣལ་འབྱོར་མེན།།

ཨིཐི།

17

Oṃ Svasti

I'm a beggar yogi
who removed external doubts through learning,
understood the meaning of reality through contemplation,
and experienced it through meditation.

When I lived for some years at home,
where evil habitual propensities are accumulated,
virtuous action was shaky.

When I went to meditate in mountain-range solitude,
I briefly encountered realization of mind itself.

When I practiced without distraction,
a continual understanding arose.

Now it doesn't depend on a state of mind.
I'm content with resolution in a birthless state.

I wander in mountain-range solitude,
or else perform sealed retreat in a cave.
If you're in the midst of an assembly, you're no yogi.

Iti

༡༨

།།ན་མོ་གུ་རུ།

ཁོ་བོས་མཁན་པ་ཁྲོད་ཀྱི་རི་རྩེར་བསྒོམས་པའི་དུས་སུ། ཉིན་ཅིག་སེམས་ཀྱི་སྣང་ཚུལ་ལ་རྟགས་པས། ཐམས་ཅད་འོ་ཀྱུལ་བར་འཕྱོང་ནས། དེའི་དུས་སུ་འདི་སྐད་ཅེས་སྨྲས་སོ།

།རྨི་ལམ་སྒྱུ་མ་དང་འདྲ་བའི་འཁོར་བ་ན། །དམུ་ལོང་སྨྱོན་པ་དང་འདྲ་བའི་སེམས་ཅན་ཅོ་འབྲམ།
།འཁྲུལ་སྣང་སྙིང་པོ་མེད་པའི་དོན་མ་རྟོགས། །རྫུན་ལ་བདེན་པར་འཛིན་ཚོ་འོ་རེ་ཀྱུལ།

།ཡང་མཚོ་མེ་ཏོག་དང་འདྲ་བའི་ཆུ་སེར་ལ། །བཅོལ་ཆུང་སྦྲང་མ་དང་འདྲ་བའི་བཞོན་པ་ཅོ་ཆགས།
།མི་རྟག་ཡལ་བ་ཅིག་ལགས་ཏེ་ངོ་མ་ཤེས། །ཐུག་མེད་ངན་སོང་དུ་འབྱམས་པ་ཅོ་འོ་རེ་ཀྱུལ།

།འཁོར་བ་མེ་དཔུང་དང་འདྲ་བའི་ཁྱིམ་ཐབ་ལ། །ཡོག་ལྷ་བྱེ་ལེབ་དང་འདྲ་བའི་ཆོས་པ་ཚོ་འབབས།
།ཐར་པའི་སྲོག་གཅོད་ཅིག་ལགས་ཏེ་ངོ་མ་ཤེས། །དུ་ཁ་བདེ་བ་རུ་འཛིན་པ་ཚོ་འོ་རེ་ཀྱུལ།

།ཚིག་ཤེས་མིག་རྒྱུ་དང་འདྲ་བའི་རྗེས་ཕྱི་རུ། །བློ་ལྡན་རི་དགས་དང་འདྲ་བའི་སྟོན་པ་ཅོ་འབྲམས།
།སྒྲ་དོན་འབྲེལ་མེད་ཅིག་ལགས་ཏེ་ངོ་མ་ཤེས། །ཐུག་མེད་ཐ་སྙད་ལ་འབྱམས་པ་ཅོ་འོ་རེ་ཀྱུལ།

།ཉམས་སྨྱོང་འཇའ་ཚོན་དང་འདྲ་བའི་བདེ་བ་ལ། །དད་ལྡན་བྱིས་པ་དང་འདྲ་བའི་སྒོམ་ཆེན་ཚོ་ཆགས།
།སླུ་ཁྲིད་གོལ་ས་ཅིག་ལགས་ཏེ་ངོ་མ་ཤེས། །དྲོད་རྟགས་འབྲས་བུར་རེ་བ་ཅོ་འོ་རེ་ཀྱུལ།

།ཅེས་འགྲོ་སྐྱོན་ཀྱི་བྲག་པ་གསུང་ངོ།།

།ཨིཐ

18

Namo Guru

When I was meditating on the mountain peak of Khenpa charnel ground, one day I examined how things appeared to my mind and saw everything as exhausting. At that time I said this:

In saṃsāra, which is like a dream and illusion,
sentient beings roam like blind lunatics.
Not realizing the truth that confused appearances have no essence,
those who cling to the false as true get so exhausted.

To the serum of youth, which is like a flower,
the young are attached like witless bees.
Not recognizing this is impermanent and fading,
those who wander in endless lower realms get so exhausted.

Into married life in saṃsāra, which is like a bonfire,
Dharma practitioners fall like moths with distorted vision.
Not recognizing that the life force of liberation is being cut,
those who cling to suffering as pleasure get so exhausted.

After word-knowledge, which is like a mirage,
teachers wander like smart wild beasts.
Not recognizing that there's no connection between term
and meaning,
those who wander in endless jargon get so exhausted.

To the pleasure of experience, which is like a rainbow,
meditators are attached like faithful children.
Not recognizing that it's an enticing dead end,
those who hope for a result of spiritual warmths and signs
get so exhausted.

Spoken by Godrakpa, the protector of living beings.

Iti

༡༨

།།ཟད་ཀྱི་སྐད་ཁུང་དུ།།

།།ན་མོ་གུ་རུ

ཨེབ་ཆོ་ཀད་ཁུང་དུ་ནུབ་ཅིག་རྨི་ལམ་ན་བྲམ་ཟེ་ཆེན་པོ་ཡིན་ཟེར་བའི་རྣལ་འབྱོར་པ་གཟི་མདངས་ཅན་ཅིག་འདི་སྐད་ཅེས་ལེན་པ་ཐོས་སོ།

།བྱ་ལྟོས་དང་ཕ་རིའི་ལོགས་ལ་ལྟོས། །ཕ་རིའི་ལོགས་ལ་ལྟས་ཙམ་ན།
།ནམ་ཟླ་ཡུད་ཀྱིས་སོང་ཙམ་ན། །སྤྲིན་ན་འུན་གྱི་འོག་ན་སྤྱང་རི་སེར།

།ལྟོས་དང་རང་གི་ལུས་ལ་ལྟོས། །རང་གི་ལུས་ལ་བལྟས་ཙམ་ན།
།ལོ་ཟླ་ཞག་གསུམ་འདས་ཙམ་ན། །མི་ཆེ་སོག་སྤུན་གྱི་ངང་ལ་ཟད།

།ལྟོས་དང་གནས་ལུགས་ཀྱི་དོན་ལ་ལྟོས། །གནས་ལུགས་ཀྱི་དོན་ལྟ་ལྟས་ཙམ་ན།
།ཡེ་ནས་རང་གསལ་ཆོས་ཀྱི་སྐུ། །སེམས་མ་བཅོས་པ་ཡི་ངང་ལ་ཞོག།

ཅེས་ཟེར་བ་རྨི་བ་དང་། ནང་པར་ནམ་ཞོ་ཆད་པ་དང་།སྤྱང་རི་ཡང་སེར་ཡོག་སོང་ནས་འདུག་ཏེ། སྟོང་པ་དང་མི་རྟག་པ་རྒྱུད་ལ་སྐྱེས་སོ།།

ཨྠི

19

At Zegyi Gekung:

Namo Guru

One night, in a dream at Ebcho Gekung, I heard a radiant yogi, who said, "I'm the Great Brahmin," sing these words:

> Look, my son! Look at the mountainside over there!
> If you just look at the mountainside over there,
> when the weather changes in a moment,
> there's a yellow alpine meadow below the clouds and mist.
>
> Look at your own body! Look!
> If you just look at your own body,
> when the years, months, and days have passed,
> a lifetime has vanished in a flash.
>
> Look at the truth of the way things really are! Look!
> If you just look at the truth of the way things really are,
> it's the primordial, naturally radiant, buddha body of reality.
> Leave the mind in that unfabricated state!

I dreamed he said that. In the morning, the rains had stopped and the alpine meadow had also turned yellow. Emptiness and impermanence arose in my mindstream.

Iti

༣༠

།།ན་མོ་གུ་རུ།

ཡང་རྗེ་རི་ལོ་པམ་དུ་སྡོས་སུ་བུད་མེད་བཟང་ཕྱུག་ཅིག་འོངས་ནས་འདི་སྐད་ཞེར་རོ།

།ཤིག་གི་སྙིང་པོ་ཆུག་དང་ལྷོ་གོ་ཟན་གྱིས་བཙོད།
།སྡེ་སྣོད་རྣམ་གསུམ་ཞེས་དང་ལག་ལེན་སྐྱེད་རྫོགས་གཉིས།

།ཅེས་ཟེར་ནས་མི་སྣང་ངོ།།

ཨྠི།།

Tingri Langkor

20

Namo Guru

Once, at Lopam on Mt. Tsi, a beautiful woman appeared beside my pillow and said this:

> Even though you are rich with gems,
> roasted barley dough is enough for food.
> Even though the three piṭakas are understood,
> the practice is both creation and perfection.

Saying that, she disappeared.

Iti

༣༡

།ན་མོ་གུ་རུ།

འཆི་བ་སེམས་ཀྱི་མེ་ལོང་ཡིན། །འཆི་རུ་འདུག་གམ་མི་འདུག་ལྟོས།
།ཇི་སྲིད་འཆི་བས་འཇིགས་ཀྱི་བར། །ད་རུང་ཅིག་ཕུར་རི་ལ་བསྒོམས།

།ན་བ་དགེ་སྦྱོར་གྱི་གསལ་འདེབས་ཡིན། །ན་རྒྱུ་འདུག་གམ་མི་འདུག་ལྟོས།
།ནད་ཇི་སྲིད་སེམས་ལ་གནོད་ཀྱི་བར། །ད་དུང་ན་མཁན་གྱི་རིག་པ་ལྟོས།

།རྐྱེན་དྲག་དད་པའི་གསལ་འདེབས་ཡིན། །ཕན་གནོད་འདུག་གམ་མི་འདུག་ལྟོས།
།རྐྱེན་ཇི་སྲིད་སེམས་ལ་གནོད་ཀྱི་བར། །ད་དུང་རྟེན་མེད་ཀྱི་སེམས་ལ་གོམས་འདྲིས་གྱིས།

།འདོད་ཡོན་ལན་ཚའི་ཆུ་སྐོད་འདྲ། །ཞིམ་པ་འདུག་གམ་མི་འདུག་ལྟོས།
།ཞེན་པ་རྟེང་ནས་མ་ལོག་ན། །ད་དུང་གཉེན་པོས་རྒྱུད་དུ་སྦྱོངས།

།ཟས་ནོར་འཆིང་བའི་ཐག་པ་ཡིན། །ཞེན་མེད་ཀྱི་གཞན་དོན་དུ་འགྲོ་འམ་ལྟོས།
།ཇི་སྲིད་འཛིན་པ་ཡོད་ཀྱི་བར། །དགོས་མེད་བློ་ཡིས་སྦྱོངས་ལ་ཐོང་།

།འགྲོ་དྲུག་དྲིན་ཅན་གྱི་ཕ་མ་ཡིན། །ཕྱོགས་རིས་འདུག་གམ་མི་འདུག་ལྟོས།
།ཇི་སྲིད་ཆགས་སྡང་ཡོད་ཀྱི་བར། །ད་དུང་ཀུན་ལ་བྱམས་པ་སྒོམ།

།ཕ་ཡུལ་འཁོར་བའི་གཏོད་ཕུར་ཡིན། །འཐེན་ཐོགས་འདུག་གམ་མི་འདུག་ལྟོས།

21

Namo Guru

Death is the mirror of mind.
Look whether or not there's anything to die.
As long as death is frightening,
keep meditating alone on the mountain.

Sickness is an admonition to virtuous action.
Look whether or not there's anything to be sick.
As long as sickness harms the mind,
keep watching the patient's intrinsic awareness.

Intense circumstances are an admonition to faith.
Look whether or not there's benefit or harm.
As long as the mind is harmed by circumstances,
keep getting used to unsupported mind.

Sensory objects are like bubbling salt water.
Look whether or not there's satisfaction.
If attachment hasn't been totally repelled,
keep casting it away by means of the antidote.

Food and wealth are binding ropes.
Look whether they benefit others without attachment.
For as long as there's grasping,
reject and discard them with the thought that they're needless.

The six types of living beings are our kind parents.
Look whether or not there's prejudice.
For as long as there's attachment and aversion,
keep cultivating love for all.

A home is the tethering stake of saṃsāra.
Look whether or not it's been extracted.

།འབྲི་བ་རྫིང་ནས་མ་ཆོད་ན། །ད་དུང་རྒྱལ་ཁམས་ཕྱོགས་མེད་བསྐོར།

།སྨན་གྲགས་བདུད་ཀྱི་ཕྱི་འཁོར་ཡིན། །ང་རྒྱལ་སྐྱེ་འམ་མི་སྐྱེ་ལྟོས།
།ནང་དུ་རློམ་སེམས་སྐྱེས་གྱུར་ན། །ད་དུང་སྦྲང་པོའི་དམན་ས་ཟུང་།

།ཡོན་ཏན་གྱི་རྩ་བ་དད་པ་ཡིན། །སྐྱོ་ཤས་འདུག་གམ་མི་འདུག་ལྟོས།
།འཁོར་བས་སྐྱོ་བ་མ་སྐྱེས་ན། །ད་དུང་དཀར་ནག་རྒྱུ་འབྲས་ལྟོས།

།གྲོལ་བར་བྱེད་པ་ཤེས་རབ་ཡིན། །ཐམས་ཅད་སྟོང་པར་ཤེས་སམ་ལྟོས།
།དངོས་པོར་འཛིན་པ་ཡོད་ཀྱི་བར། །འཛིན་མཁན་གྱི་རིག་པ་རྟན་ལ་ཐོབ།

ཨྠི།།

If craving hasn't been totally severed,
keep roaming aimlessly around the land.

Fame is the flattery of Māra.
Look whether or not pride arises.
If conceit has arisen within,
keep holding the humble role of a beggar.

The root of good qualities is faith.
Look whether or not there's weariness.
If weariness with saṃsāra hasn't arisen,
keep watching white and black cause and result.

Transcendent knowledge is liberating.
Look whether everything has been understood to be empty.
For as long as there's grasping at things,
establish the intrinsic awareness of the grasper.

Iti

༣༣

བླ་བྲང་འོག་གི་ཐིག་ཁང་དུ།

།།ན་མོ་གུ་རུ།

སི་ཧི་ཕ་ལ་མ།

།ཐོས་པ་ཆུའི་རི་མོ་འདྲ། །བསམས་པ་སྐྱིག་རྡོས་ཀྱི་རི་མོ་འདྲ།
།སྒོམ་པ་རྡོའི་རི་མོ་འདྲ།

།ཁྱད་མཁན་བུ་མོ་བདར་དང་འདྲ། །གཞན་དག་རྩེ་བར་བདར་ནུས་སྟེ།
།བདར་ནི་ནམ་ཕུགས་སྐྱེང་པར་འཆག།

།མ་སྒོམས་ཆོས་ཀྱང་དེ་དང་འདྲ།།

ཨྠི།།

22

At the chapel of the lower residence:

Namo Guru

Siddhi Phalam

Learning is like a design in water,
contemplation like a design on the side of a wall,
meditation like a design in stone.

Like an inquisitive girl,
a teacher may be able to inquire closely about others
but, if inquired about in return, may eventually become embarrassed.

Dharma not meditated on is like that.

Iti

༣༣

ན་མོ་གུ་རུ།

བླ་མ་རྣམས་ལ་ཕྱག་འཚལ་ལོ།

།དམ་པ་ཆོས་ཀྱི་སྒོར་ཞུགས་ནས། །བློ་འདི་ཀ་རང་ལ་སྐྱིད་མེད་ན།
།བླ་མེད་ཀྱི་བྱང་ཆུབ་ཐོབ་པ་བས། །སླར་ལ་ངན་སོང་གསུམ་དུ་འབྲུམས།

།སྒྱུ་ལུས་འདི་ཡང་སྡུག་སྲན་ཆུང་། །དཀའ་ཐུབ་མི་ནུས་ཉལ་ལ་དགའ།
།ཡང་དག་དོན་ཅིག་མ་རྟོགས་ན། །ཇི་ཙམ་ཉལ་ཀྱིན་གཉིད་ལོག་ཀྱང་།
།གཏི་མུག་གི་གཉིད་ལ་སངས་དུས་མེད།

།དེ་བས་ཡར་ལོངས་སེམས་ལ་ལྟོས། །སྒྲོན་མེ་ལྟ་བུའི་རྣལ་འབྱོར་མཛོད།
།སེམས་གསལ་འགྲིབ་མེད་པའི་ངང་ལ་ཞོག།

།སྡུག་མཆུ་འདི་ཡང་སྨྲ་ལ་དགའ། །ཁ་རོག་མི་འདུག་ལོག་པ་སྨྲ།
།ངག་ཀླེང་བྲལ་གྱི་དོན་ཅིག་མ་རྟོགས་ན། །ཇི་ཙམ་འཁྲུལ་པའི་གཏམ་སྨྲས་ཀྱང་།
།ཚིག་གི་མཐའ་ལ་ཐུག་མེད་ཀྱིས།

།དེ་བས་ངག་གི་སྨྲ་བ་ཆོད། །ལྐུགས་པ་ལྟ་བུའི་རྣལ་འབྱོར་མཛོད།
།ངག་ཀླེང་བརྗོད་མེད་པའི་ངང་ལ་ཞོག།

།རང་སེམས་འདི་ཡང་མགོ་གཙོལ་ཆུང་། །བཞག་སར་མི་སྡོད་ལོག་པར་འགྲོ།
།ཉག་གཅིག་བཙད་ནས་མ་ཆོད་ན། །ཇི་ཙམ་ཡུལ་ལ་སྦྱོས་བྱས་ཀྱང་།
།འཁྲུལ་པའི་བློ་ལ་ཐུག་མེད་ཀྱིས།

23

Namo Guru

Homage to the masters.

Having entered the gate of the excellent Dharma,
if it isn't produced in this very mind,
instead of gaining unsurpassed enlightenment,
again we'll wander in the three lower realms.

This illusory body, with so little tolerance,
is incapable of hardship and fond of sleep.
If the perfect truth isn't realized,
no matter how often we wake from slumber,
the sleep of ignorance will never be removed.

So get up and watch the mind.
Practice the lamplike yoga.
Leave the mind in a radiant, unobscured state.

These pretty lips that like to speak
  aren't silent but speak falsely.
If the meaning beyond verbal description isn't realized,
no matter how much confused conversation is spoken,
the end of words will never be reached.

So stop the voice's speech.
Practice the mutelike yoga.
Leave the voice in a speechless state.

Even this mind itself is unreliable,
not staying where it's put but going wrong.
If this alone isn't totally stopped,
no matter how much it goes out to objects,
confused mind will never end.

།དེ་བས་ཡིད་ཀྱི་འགྱུ་བ་ཆོད། །ནམ་མཁའ་ལྟ་བུའི་རྒྱལ་འཁོར་མཛོད།
།སེམས་མཐའ་དབུས་མེད་པའི་ངང་ལ་ཞོག

།ཐྀ༎

So stop the circulation of thoughts.
Practice the skylike yoga.
Leave the mind in a state without limit or center.

Iti

༣༨

གླང་འཁོར་དུ།

ན་མོ་གུ་རུ།

བདག་རང་འདོད་ཀྱི་ཐག་པ་ཡལ་ནས་གདའ། །ཕན་སེམས་ཀྱི་སྤྲིན་ཕུང་འཐིབས་ནས་གདའ།
།འགྲོ་དོན་གྱི་སྦྲང་ཆར་འབབ་གིན་གདའ།

།ཉམས་ལེན་གྱི་ཡུར་ཆུང་ཀྱི་ཐོན་ཙ་ན། །རྟོགས་པའི་འབྲུ་དྲུག་སྨིན་པ་ངེས།
།མཛད་མེད་ཀྱི་སྲིས་ལ་སྤྱོད་ལ་ཆེ།

།ཆོས་འདི་ཀུན་བསམས་ཀྱིན་ཉམས་རེ་དགའ། །དབེན་པ་བྲུ་བ་ཆོག་ལ་ཆེ།
།སང་ནང་པར་སླན་ཧླེ་བརྟུང་ལས་ཆེ།

།ཞེས་དབེན་པ་ལ་བཞུགས་ཙ་ན་བཞེས་སོ།།

ཐྱི།།

24

At Langkor:

Namo Guru

The drought of my own desires has vanished.
The cloud banks of helpful intentions have gathered.
The drizzle of benefit to living beings is falling.

When the little weeds of practice have been pulled,
the six grains of realization will certainly ripen.
Surely the inexhaustible nectar will be enjoyed.

Thinking of all this Dharma, I'm so delighted.
Surely content living in solitude.
Surely I'll strike the gong tomorrow morning.

Sung while staying in solitude.

Iti

༣༥

།ན་མོ་གུ་རུ།

ཨོཾ་མ་ཎི་པདྨེ་ཧཱུྃ།

།ཕྱི་གཟུང་བའི་ཡུལ་ཀྱང་ནམ་མཁའ་བཞིན། །ནང་འཛིན་པའི་སེམས་དང་ནམ་མཁའ་བཞིན།
།དོན་མཐའ་དབུས་མེད་པའི་སྟོང་ཤེད་ན། །ཆོས་ལྟ་བའི་ཐག་ཆོད་བློ་རེ་བདེ།

།ཕྱི་གཟུང་བའི་ཡུལ་དང་ཉི་ཟླ་བཞིན། །ནང་འཛིན་པའི་སེམས་དང་ཉི་ཟླ་བཞིན།
།དོན་གསལ་འགྲིབ་མེད་པའི་སྟོང་ཤེད་ན། །ཆོས་སྒོམ་པའི་ཐག་ཆོད་བློ་རེ་བདེ།

།ཕྱི་གཟུང་བའི་ཡུལ་ཡང་རི་བོ་བཞིན། །ནང་འཛིན་པའི་སེམས་དང་རི་བོ་བཞིན།
།དོན་འཕོ་འགྱུར་མེད་པའི་སྟོང་ཤེད་ན། །ཆོས་སྤྱོད་པའི་ཐག་ཆོད་བློ་རེ་བདེ།

།ཕྱི་གཟུང་བའི་ཡུལ་ཡང་མེ་དཔུང་བཞིན། །ནང་འཛིན་པའི་སེམས་དང་བཙའ་འཕྲུང་བཞིན།
།འཛོམ་དོགས་གཉིས་ཀྱི་སྟོང་ཤེད་ན། །ཆོས་དམ་ཚིག་གི་ཐག་ཆོད་བློ་རེ་བདེ།

།ཕྱི་གཟུང་བའི་ཡུལ་ཡང་གཏེར་སྦས་བཞིན། །ནང་འཛིན་པའི་སེམས་དང་གཏེར་སྟེད་བཞིན།
།གཏེར་སྦས་གཏེར་སྟེད་གཉིས་ཀྱི་སྟོང་ཤེད་ན། །ཆོས་འབྲས་བུའི་ཐག་ཆོད་བློ་རེ་བདེ།།

ཨིཐི།།

25

Namo Guru

Oṃ Maṇi Padme Hūṃ

External apprehended objects like the sky.
Internal apprehending mind also like the sky.
In a state of truth without limit or center,
I'm so content in the resolution of the view of Dharma.

External apprehended objects like the sun and moon.
Internal apprehending mind also like the sun and moon.
In a state of radiant and unobscured truth,
I'm so content in the resolution of the meditation of Dharma.

External apprehended objects like a mountain.
Internal apprehending mind also like a mountain.
In a state of immutable truth,
I'm so content in the resolution of the conduct of Dharma.

External apprehended objects like a bonfire.
Internal apprehending mind like a narrow pathway.
In a state of both restraint and fear,
I'm so content in the resolution of the sacred commitments
of Dharma.

External apprehended objects like hidden treasure.
Internal apprehending mind like discovered treasure.
In a state of both hidden and discovered treasure,
I'm so content in the resolution of the result of Dharma.

Iti

༣༨

ལྟིམ་ལུངས་ལུང་སྒྲོད་གྱི་རི་ཁར།

།ན་མོ་གུ་རུ།

ཤུ་ཁ་བོའི་གངས་ལ་ལྟ་ལྟ་ནས། །མདའ་རུལ་ཀྱུ་འདུག་པ་མ་ཚོར་རོ།
།ཡར་སོ་ནམ་བྱ་བ་འཕྱིས་ལ་ཆེ།

།ཡོགས་རམ་བའི་རྫ་ལ་བལྟ་ལྟ་ནས། །ཀླུངས་སྟེ་ཐོག་རྒྱས་པ་མ་ཚོར་རོ།
།འཚོ་སྐྱོང་བྱ་བ་འཕྱིས་ལས་བྱེ།

།མདའ་ནི་གསེང་སྒོ་ལ་བལྟ་ལྟ་ནས། །ཤུ་སྦྱང་ཁ་སེར་བ་མ་ཚོར་རོ།
།སྟོན་ཐོག་སྡུ་བ་འཕྱིས་ལ་ཆེ།

།ཚེ་འདི་དོན་དུ་གཉེར་གཉེར་ནས། །ལུས་རྒས་ཞིས་བཏུགས་པ་མ་ཚོར་རོ།
།ལྟ་ཆོས་བྱ་བ་འཕྱིས་ལས་ཆེ།

།དཔེ་བཞི་དོན་ལྡོག།

ཨྠི།།

26

On the mountain peak of Jimlung Lungdrö:

Namo Guru

Watching—watching the Khawo glacier in the upper valley,
the meltwater in the lower valley wasn't noticed.
It's too late for cultivation.

Watching—watching the clay slopes of Rumbu,
the daisies spread on the valley floor weren't noticed.
It's too late to tend the herds.

Watching—watching the green rushes in the lower valley,
the yellow meadow of the upper valley wasn't noticed.
It's too late to gather the autumn harvest.

Striving—striving for the aims of this life,
the body aging and approaching death wasn't noticed.
It's too late to practice the divine Dharma.

There are four examples and five points.

Iti

༣༤

།གླང་འཁོར་དུ།

།ན་མོ་གུ་རུ།

མི་ང་དང་ཀ་ལ་ཧྨ་ཀ་གཉིས། །དགུན་གསུམ་ནགས་ཀྱི་ཁྲོད་ན་བདེ།
།གཅན་ཟན་མེད་དེ་ཞིན་དུ་བདེ།

།ང་དང་ལྷོག་ཆུང་ཀྱུར་མོ་གཉིས། །དཔྱིད་གསུམ་ན་མའི་འདྲམ་ན་བདེ།
།སོ་ནམ་མེད་དེ་ཞིན་དུ་བདེ།

།ང་དང་ལྷ་བྱ་གོང་མོ་གཉིས། །དབྱར་གསུམ་སྤང་རིའི་ངོས་ན་བདེ།
།བེ་ལུག་མེད་དེ་ཞིན་དུ་བདེ།

།ང་དང་རི་བྱ་སྲེག་པ་གཉིས། །སྟོན་གསུམ་རིའི་སུལ་ན་བདེ།
།ཇུས་གཡུལ་མེད་དེ་ཞིན་དུ་བདེ།

།ཆོས་བྱེད་ཀྱི་ཞེས་པ་ནམ་ཡང་བདེ།

།དུས་བཞི་དང་མཐུན་པའི་གླུའོ།།

27

At Langkor:

Namo Guru

Both the nightingale and I
  are happy in the midst of the forest for the three months of
    winter,
so very happy where there are no beasts of prey.

Both the swallow and I
  are happy at the edge of a marsh for the three months of spring,
so very happy where there's no cultivation.

Both the white grouse and I
  are happy on the slope of an alpine meadow
    for the three months of summer,
so very happy where there are no young yaks and lambs.

Both the alpine partridge and I
  are happy in the mountain ravines for the three months of
    autumn,
so very happy where there's no cutting and threshing.

Completely happy with the knowledge that I'm practicing Dharma.

A song corresponding to the four seasons.

༣༥

ནམོ་གུ་རུ།

རྗེ་རིན་པོ་ཆེ་ཟླ་འཁོར་ན་འདུག་ཁ་ལ་བཞུགས་དུས། ནུབ་གཅིག་དུང་དུ་མཁའ་འགྲོ་མ་ཅིག་བྱུང་ནས། འཆམ་ཀྱིན་འདི་སྐད་ཅེས་གསུང་ངོ་།

།ང་ནམ་མཁའ་འཐོངས་ཀྱི་མཁའ་འགྲོ་མ། །བཞུགས་ནི་རི་རབ་ཀྱི་འཐོངས་ལ་བཞུགས།

།ང་དུ་ཁྲོད་རྒྱུད་ཀྱི་མཁའ་འགྲོ་མ། །ཁྱབ་ནི་འཛམ་གླིང་ཀུན་དུ་ཁྱབ།

།ང་ཨུ་རྒྱན་ཡུལ་གྱི་མཁའ་འགྲོ་མ། །སྐྱོབ་ནི་ལས་ཅན་བྱིན་གྱིས་བརླབ།

།ཅེས་གསུང་པ་ལ། རིན་པོ་ཆེས་འདི་སྐད་ཅེས་ལན་དུ་གསུངས་སོ།

།མཁའ་འགྲོ་མ་རྣམས་རིང་ནས་འདུས། །ཉམས་བདེ་བ་ཆེན་པོར་བྱིན་གྱིས་བརླབས།

།མཁའ་འགྲོ་མ་རྣམས་རིང་ནས་འདུས། །རྣལ་འབྱོར་བདག་ལ་བདེ་ཆེན་སྟོར།

།མཁའ་འགྲོ་མ་རྣམས་རིང་ནས་འདུས། །སྒྲུབ་པ་པོའི་བར་ཆད་སོལ།

།ཅེས་གསུངས་སོ།།

མཁའ་འགྲོ་མའི་འཕུར་དབྱངས་ཞུས་ལན་མ་ལགས་སོ།

།ཨིཐི།།

28

Namo Guru

When the precious lord was staying in sealed retreat at Langkor, ḍākinīs appeared before him one night and said this while dancing:

> I'm the ḍākinī of the heights of the sky.
> For a residence I reside in the heights above Mt. Meru.
>
> I'm the ḍākinī of the eight charnel grounds.
> For a range I range through all the Jambu continent.
>
> I'm the ḍākinī of the land of Uḍḍiyana.
> For a blessing I bless those with the karma.

So they spoke. The precious one said this in reply:

> Ḍākinīs gathered from afar,
> bless me with the experience of great bliss!
>
> Ḍākinīs gathered from afar,
> ignite great bliss in me, the yogi!
>
> Ḍākinīs gathered from afar,
> remove a meditator's obstacles!

So he spoke.

This is the song of the ḍākinīs in flight, and the reply.

Iti

༣༩

དེའི་དུས་ན་འདག་ཀ་བཞི་དགུ་ཡོད།།

ན་མོ་གུ་རུ།

ཟླ་འཁོར་ན་འདག་ཁ་ལ་བཞུགས་པའི་དུས་སུ་བཞེས་པ།

བདག་དང་པོ་ཡུལ་ན་ཡོད་ཙ་ན། །གདུགས་ཉི་མ་གཟའ་ཡིས་ཟིན་པ་བཞིན།
།སྣང་བ་ཀྲག་མེད་དུ་ཤར་བའི་ཉམས་ཅིག་ཤར། །དེ་དད་པ་གཏིང་ནས་སྐྱེས་པར་གདའ།

།དེ་ནས་ལོ་འགའ་ལོན་ཙ་ན། །མཚོ་འཁྲུགས་གི་སྟེང་ན་བྱ་བབས་བཞིན།
།གང་ལ་ཡང་ཞེན་མེད་ཀྱི་ཉམས་ཅིག་ཤར། །དེ་ཞེན་པ་གཏིང་ནས་ལོག་པར་གདའ།

།དེ་ནས་བླ་མའི་དྲུང་དུ་བཏུད་ཙམ་ན། །འཇིགས་སར་སྐྱེལ་མ་རྙེད་པ་བཞིན།
།བློ་ལྟོས་འཆའ་བའི་ཉམས་ཅིག་ཤར། །དེ་མོས་གུས་གཉིང་ནས་ཆུད་པར་གདའ།

།དེ་ནས་ཟབ་མོའི་གདམས་ངག་ཐོབ་ཙམ་ན། །སྔར་འདྲིས་ཀྱི་མི་དང་ཕྲད་པ་བཞིན།
།བློ་ཐེ་ཚོམ་དང་བྲལ་བའི་ཉམས་ཅིག་ཤར། །དེ་ཡིད་ཆེས་གཉིང་ནས་སྐྱེས་པར་གདའ།

།གཅིག་པུར་ཉམས་སུ་ལེན་དུས་སུ། །རི་དགས་ཀྱི་རྒྱལ་པོ་གསེ་རུ་བཞིན།
།རང་ཅིག་པུར་བདེ་བའི་ཉམས་ཅིག་ཤར། །དེ་དོན་ལ་ངེས་ཤེས་སྐྱེས་པར་གདའ།

།སེམས་ཅན་གྱི་འགྲོ་དོན་བྱེད་དུས་སུ། །མ་ཡིས་བུ་གཅིག་པོ་མཐོང་བ་འཞིན།
།ཡིད་གདུང་བ་དང་བཅས་པའི་ཉམས་ཅིག་ཤར། །དེ་བྱམས་སྙིང་རྗེ་སྙིང་ནས་སྐྱེས་པར་གདའ།

29

At that time there were forty-nine in sealed retreat.

Namo Guru

Sung while staying in sealed retreat at Langkor:

At first, when I was still at home,
like the heavenly sun eclipsed by Rāhu,
an experience of muted appearances dawned.
That was the deep birth of faith.

Then, several years passed,
and like a bird landing upon a frozen lake,
an experience of no attachment to anything dawned.
That was the deep repudiation of attachment.

Then, while bowing in the presence of the master,
like finding an escort in a dangerous place,
an experience of mental assurance dawned.
That was the deep penetration of devotion.

Then, while receiving the profound oral instructions,
like meeting a familiar person from before,
an experience of freedom from mental doubts dawned.
That was the deep birth of belief.

While practicing alone,
like the rhinoceros who is king of wild beasts,
an experience of being happy alone dawned.
That was the birth of certainty in the meaning.

While working for the benefit of sentient beings,
like a mother seeing an only child,
an experience of tenderness dawned.
That was the heartfelt birth of love and compassion.

།རི་ཁྲོད་དབེན་པ་འགྲིམས་དུས་སུ། །གཅན་ཟན་གྱི་རྒྱལ་པོ་སེང་གེ་བཞིན།
།བློ་ཉམས་ང་དང་བྲལ་བའི་ཉམས་ཅིག་ཤར། །དེ་བདེར་ཆེན་ཁོང་དུ་ཆུད་པར་གདའ།།

།ཅེས་གསུངས་སོ།།

ཨི་ཐི།།

While wandering in isolated mountain ranges,
like the lion who is king of the beasts of prey,
an experience of fearless mind dawned.
That was the mastery of great confidence.

So he spoke.

Iti

༣༠

ན་མོ་གུ་རུ།

ཡང་དེའི་དུས་སུ་འདི་ཡང་གསུངས་སོ།

གཡར་གསུམ་སྤང་ལ་ཆུ་མིག་རྫོལ། །སེམས་སྐྱེ་མེད་ངང་ལ་མི་གནས་པར།
།ཉམས་རྟོག་ཐོལ་སྐྱེས་སུ་འོང་བའི་དཔེ་རུ་གདའོ།

།སྟོན་གསུམ་རྩྭའི་སྦོ་ཐག་ཆད། །ཡོ་ཟླ་ཞག་གསུམ་འདས་པ་ན།
།གཞོན་ལང་མཚོ་ཡལ་བའི་དཔེ་རུ་གདའོ།

།དགུན་གསུམ་ཆུ་བོ་སྦུབས་སུ་ཞུགས། །སེམས་ཆོས་ཉིད་ཀྱི་དོན་ལ་བལྟས་ཙམ་ན།
།ཀླུང་སེམས་རྡོ་ཡི་ཟིན་པའི་དཔེ་རུ་གདའོ།

།དཔྱིད་གསུམ་གངས་ལ་ཞུན་ཆུ་གྲུབ། །འབྲུ་དུག་གང་བཏབ་སྨིན་ཙམ་ན།
།རྒྱུ་འབྲས་གང་བཏབ་སྨིན་པའི་གདའ་རུ་གདའོ།

།དུས་བཞིའི་དབྱངས

ཨིཐི༎

30

Namo Guru

This was also spoken at that time:

Springs erupt in the meadows during the three months of summer.
This is a metaphor for the eruption of thoughts
while the mind isn't resting in the birthless state.

Green grass withers during the three months of autumn.
This is a metaphor for the fading of youthful vitality
while the years, months, and days pass.

Streams enter hollows during the three months of winter.
This is a metaphor for the natural arresting of the vital winds and
mind while the true nature of mind is being watched.

Meltwater floods from the glaciers during the three months
of spring.
This is a metaphor for the result ripening from whichever cause
was planted,
just like the ripening of whichever of the six grains was sown.

A song of the four seasons.

Iti

༄༅

།ན་མོ་གུ་རུ།

གཡོག་འཁོར་དུ་འཇོམ་པའི་སྤྱི་དཔོན་ལ། །གཞན་ཕྱོགས་མེད་དུ་འཁྲོག་པའི་ཁ་དྲག་གདའ་ཏེ། །དེས་དམྱལ་བའི་བསྐྱུངས་མ་མི་ཟློགས་པར་གདའ། །འ་རང་ཕན་སེམས་བསྐྱེད་པའི་ལྷ་ཆོས་ལ་གཞིགས་སམ།

།ནོར་རྫས་སོག་འཇོག་ལ་མཁས་པའི་ཕྱུག་པོ་ཚོ་ལ། །ད་ལྟ་སྐྱིད་ན་བདེ་བའི་ཟས་ནོར་གདའ་སྟེ། །དེས་ཡིད་དགས་ཀྱི་བཀྲེས་སྐོམ་མི་སྐྱོབས་པར་གདའ་སྟེ། །འ་རང་རྫས་ཚོགས་སུ་བཏོངས་པའི་ལྷ་ཆོས་ལ་གཞིགས་སམ།

།རིགས་རྒྱུད་ཀྱི་མཐོ་བའི་རྗེ་བཙན་ཚོ་ལ། །ཀུན་གྱིས་འོག་དུ་འཛུལ་བའི་ཁུར་ཚད་གདའ་ཏེ། །རང་འཆི་བའི་དུས་ན་གཅིག་པུར་འགྲོ་བར་གདའ་སྟེ། །འ་རང་དམའ་ས་འཛིན་པའི་ལྷ་ཆོས་ལ་གཞིགས་སམ།

།བློ་ཤེས་རབ་དང་ལྡན་པའི་སྟོན་ཆེན་ལ། །ཕྱི་ཐོས་པ་ཚིག་གི་ལོ་མ་གདའ་སྟེ། །ནང་སེམས་ཀྱི་རྩ་བ་མ་མཐོང་བར་གདའ་ཡི། །འ་རང་དོན་ཉམས་སུ་ལེན་པའི་ལྷ་ཆོས་ལ་གཞིགས་སམ།

།སྐུ་བསོད་ནམས་དང་ལྡན་པའི་དགེ་ཤེས་ཚོ་ལ། །ནམ་བཟའ་བསྐོན་འབུད་བྱེད་པའི་གཟིམས་གཡོག་པ་གདའ་སྟེ། །སྲིད་པ་བར་དོར་གཟིམས་གཡོག་པ་མི་ཡོང་བར་གདའ་ཡི། འ་རང་དཔོན་མེད་གཡོག་མེད་ཀྱི་ལྷ་ཆོས་ལ་གཞིགས་སམ།

།གནས་རྒྱ་ཤིང་འཇོམ་པའི་དགོན་པ་ན། །འཐུན་རྐྱེན་དང་ལྡན་པའི་སོ་སོང་གདའ་སྟེ།

31

Namo Guru

For rulers with servants gathered as a retinue,
there's aimless barking at others with harsh speech.
But that won't turn back the guardians of hell.
Have you come to our divine Dharma of developing
beneficial intentions?

For the rich who are skilled at gathering and hoarding valuables,
there's food and wealth that's pleasant if used now.
But that won't save you from the hunger and thirst
of the hungry ghosts.
Have you come to our divine Dharma of giving things away
to the assembly?

For the high lords of hereditary lines,
everyone has the burden of being subservient.
But at the time of death you'll go alone.
Have you come to our divine Dharma of assuming a humble role?

For great teachers endowed with intellectual knowledge,
there are leaves of the words of external study,
but the root of internal mind isn't seen.
Have you come to our divine Dharma of practicing the meaning?

For prosperous spiritual friends,
there are valets for putting on and removing attire.
But there won't be valets in the intermediate state
of existence.
Have you come to our divine Dharma that has no lords
and no servants?

At a secluded site of clustered plantain trees,
favorable conditions are hoarded.

།ཡུན་རིངས་སུ་བསྟུད་ཡོང་མི་གདའ་ཡི། །འུ་རང་རི་ཁྲོད་འགྲིམས་པའི་ལྷ་ཆོས་ལ་གཤེགས་སམ།

།ཉང་སྟོད་བསོད་ནམས་སྤྱིངས་ཁྱུང་དུ། །གནས་བྱིན་གྱི་བརླབས་པའི་ཀོ་བྲག་ཏུ།
།མ་མཁའ་འགྲོ་འདུ་བའི་གནས་ཆེན་དུ། །ཉོན་མོངས་པ་བླུ་བའི་གླུ་འདི་བླངས་སོ།།

ཨིཐི།།

But they won't last long.
Have you come to our divine Dharma of wandering
 the mountain ranges?

On the little ridge of merit in Upper Nyang,
at the blessed site of Godrak,
at the holy place where the mother ḍākinīs gather,
this song to trick the afflicting emotions was sung.

Iti

༣༣

ན་མོ་གུ་རུ།

རྗེ་རིན་པོ་ཆེས་སྐྱིད་གྲོང་ཇོ་བོ་ཐུགས་རྗེ་ཆེན་པོ་གཟིགས་སུ་བྱོན་ཙ་ན། །དགུན་གྱི་ལུང་པར་བུད་མེད་ཡུར་མ་ཡུར་བ་ཚོ་ཅིག་ན་རེ། རྒྱལ་འབྱོར་པ་ཁྱེད་ད་ནང་གང་ནས་བྱོན། ད་ནུབ་གང་དུ་འགྲོ། །སྐྱོ་རོགས་སུ་ནི་སུ་ཅིག་ཡོད། །ལྟུན་དུ་ཁོ་ན་ཅི་ཞིག་འདིངས། །གོས་སུ་ཁོ་ན་ཅི་ཞིག་གོན། །ཐུས་སུ་ཁོ་ན་ཅི་ཞིག་འཐུང། འགྲོགས་པའི་གྲོགས་སུ་སུ་ཅིག་འགྲོགས། །ཟས་སུ་ཁོ་ན་ཅི་ཞིག་ཟ། །སྐོམ་དུ་ཁོ་ན་ཅི་ཞིག་འཐུང། །ཞེས་ཟེར་རོ།།
དེའི་ལན་དུ་རྗེ་རིན་པོ་ཆེ་པས་འདི་སྐད་ཅེས་གསུངས་སོ།།

> ངེད་ད་ནང་ཆོས་ཀྱི་དབྱིངས་ནས་འོངས།
> །ད་ནུབ་ཆོས་ཀྱི་དབྱིངས་སུ་འགྲོ།
> །སྐྱོ་རོགས་བླ་མའི་གདམས་ངག་ཡོད།
> །ལྟན་དུ་བདེ་བ་ཆེན་པོ་འདིངས།
> །གོས་སུ་གཏུམ་མའི་རང་དྲོད་གོན།
> །ཐུས་སུ་སྙམ་པ་ཆེན་པོ་འཛུད།
> །གྲོགས་སུ་རང་རིག་གྲོགས་དང་འགྲོགས།
> །ཟས་སུ་ཏིང་འཛིན་དག་པ་ཟ།
> །སྐོམ་ལ་རྒྱུན་ཆད་མེད་པ་འཐུང།
> །ཟས་ནི་གཉིས་སུ་མེད་པར་ཟོས།
> །རོ་ནི་བདེ་བ་ཆེན་པོར་མྱོང།
> །དོན་གྱི་སྐུ་གསུམ་མངོན་འགྱུར་འགྱུབ།

ཅེས་གསུངས་པས། མཆེད་པོ་བླ་མ་མཁའ་འགྲོ་དང་གཉིས་ལ་ཁོ་པ་དད་ནས། ཚོགས་མང་པོ་དྲངས་སོ།།

ཨྠི།།

32

Namo Guru

When the precious lord went to see the Lord of Great Compassion at Gyirong, one of the women pulling weeds in the valley of Gün asked, "Yogi, where did you come from this morning? Where will you go tonight? Who do you have for a friend when you're sad? What do you spread out as a seat? What do you wear for clothing? What do you use for a pillow? Who are you friendly with as a close companion? What do you eat for food? What do you drink for a drink?"

In reply to her, the precious lord said this:

> This morning I came from the expanse of reality.
> Tonight I'll go into the expanse of reality.
> I have the master's oral instructions for a friend when I'm sad.
> I spread out great bliss as a seat.
> I wear the natural warmth of the primordial for clothing.
> I use great equanimity for a pillow.
> I'm friendly with intrinsic self-awareness
> as a close companion.
> I eat pure meditative concentration for food.
> I drink continuity for a drink.
> The food is eaten in nonduality,
> the taste experienced as great bliss.
> The actualization of the three true buddha bodies is achieved.

When he said this, they gained faith in both him and the brother Lama Khandro and served them much food.

Iti

༣༣

།།ན་མོ་གུ་རུ།

གཟུང་བའི་ཡུལ་མེད་དོ། །རྒྱལ་ཁམས་ཕྱོགས་མེད་བསྐོར།
།ད་ལྟ་གཏན་ཡུལ་སེམས་ལ་རྙེད་པའི་རྣལ་འབྱོར་རང་སྐྱིད་དོ།

།རྟོགས་པའི་མཁར་མེད་དོ། །བསམས་རྟན་ཉམས་ཀྱི་མཁར།
།གཡེང་བའི་དམག་དཔུང་བཟློག་པའི་རྣལ་འབྱོར་པ་རང་སྐྱིད་དོ།

།བསགས་པའི་ནོར་མེད་དོ། །ཆོག་ཤེས་ནང་ནས་ཤར།
།ད་ལྟ་མཛད་མེད་གཏེར་ལ་སྤྱོད་པའི་རྣལ་འབྱོར་པ་རང་སྐྱིད་དོ།

།འགྲོགས་དཔའི་གྲོགས་མེད་དོ། །གཉུག་མ་ཡིད་ཀྱི་གྲོགས།
།ཆོས་ཉིད་འདུ་འབྲལ་མེད་པའི་རྣལ་འབྱོར་པ་སྐྱིད་དོ།

།ཚེ་འཕུང་བུ་མེད་དོ། །རིག་པ་ཁྲིའུ་སྲས།
།རྒྱལ་བའི་གདུང་རྒྱུད་འཛིན་པའི་རྣལ་འབྱོར་པ་སྐྱིད་དོ།

།གསོལ་བའི་ལྷ་མེད་དོ། །བླ་མ་དཀོན་མཆོག་གསུམ།
།མོས་གུས་འདུ་འབྲལ་མེད་པའི་རྣལ་འབྱོར་རང་སྐྱིད་དོ།།

ཨིཐི།།

33

Namo Guru

No home to uphold;
just roaming aimlessly through the land.
Now the yogi who has discovered the mind as a permanent home
is so happy.

No constructed castle;
just the castle of experiencing mental stability.
The yogi who has turned back the militant hordes of distraction
is so happy.

No accumulated wealth;
just contentment that dawns from within.
Now the yogi who enjoys an inexhaustible treasure
is so happy.

No friendly companion;
just the companion of primordial mind.
The yogi who never parts from the true nature
is so happy.

No son in this short life;
just the infant of intrinsic awareness.
The yogi who upholds the hereditary line of the Victors
is so happy.

No supplicated deity;
just the master and the Three Jewels.
The yogi who never parts from devotion
is so happy.

Iti

༣༨

།།ན་མོ་གུ་རུ།།

རྗེ་རིན་པོ་ཆེས་གདུང་ཁང་ཤུས་ནས། སྙིང་རྗེ་ཁང་བུ་གཉིས་པོ་ཕུབ་པའི་དུས་སུ། མགུར་འདི་བཞེས་པ།

ཕ་ཡུལ་ཟླུག་ཁང་བཞིན་དུ་བསྒྲུང་བསྒྲུང་ནས། །འགྲོན་ཁང་བཞིན་དུ་འབོར་འབོར་འདུག
།ཡུལ་ལ་ཕྱུགས་ཞེན་མ་སྐྱེས་པས། །ད་ལྟ་རྒྱལ་ཁམས་བསྐོར་བ་དེ་ཚུག་ལགས་སོ།

།ཁང་པ་རྡོ་བཟོ་བཞིན་དུ་སྒྲུབ་སྒྲུབ་ནས། །རྡོ་ཆག་བཞིན་དུ་འདོར་འདོར་འདུག
།བདག་གནས་ལ་ཞེན་པ་མ་སྐྱེས་པས། །ད་ལྟ་ཁང་པ་འགྲོན་དུ་བཏོང་བ་དེ་ལྟར་ལགས་སོ།

།རང་ལུས་སྐྱེ་ཤིང་བཞིན་དུ་བསྒྲུང་བསྒྲུང་ནས། །སྒོང་གོག་བཞིན་དུ་འབོར་འབོར་འདུག
།བདག་ལུས་ལ་ཆགས་ཞེན་མ་སྐྱེས་པས། །ད་ལྟ་དམན་ཆ་འཛིན་པ་དེ་ལྟར་ལགས་སོ།

།ཉེ་འབྲེལ་ཕྱུགས་རང་བཞིན་དུ་སྐྱོང་སྐྱོང་ནས། །ཚོང་འདུས་འགྲོན་པོ་བཞིན་དུ་འགྲེས་འགྲེས་འདུག
།བདག་གཉེན་ལ་ཆགས་ཞེན་མ་སྐྱེས་པས། །འབྲེལ་པ་གོད་དུ་གཅོད་པ་དེ་ཚུག་ལགས་སོ།

།ཟས་ནོར་ཁོང་ཁྲག་བཞིན་དུ་སྤྱིང་སྤྱིང་ནས། །སླབས་ལུད་བཞིན་དུ་འདོར་འདོར་འདུག
།བདག་ནོར་ལ་ཆགས་ཞེན་མ་སྐྱེས་པས། །རྫས་ཚོགས་སུ་བཏང་བ་དེ་ལྟར་ལགས་སོ།

34

Namo Guru

When the precious lord was compassionately building two small houses modeled on a residence, he sang this song:

After guarding—guarding the home as if it were the house
   of the body,
it'll just be abandoned—abandoned like a guesthouse.
Obsessive attachment to a home hasn't arisen for me,
which is why I now roam the land.

After tending—tending to a house as if fashioning clay,
it'll just be discarded—discarded like a broken pot.
Obsessive attachment to a place hasn't arisen for me,
which is why I now donate these houses for guests.

After guarding—guarding your own body as if it were a
   living tree,
it'll just be abandoned—abandoned like a rotten log.
Obsessive attachment to the body hasn't arisen for me,
which is why I now assume a humble role.

After caring—caring for relatives as if they were cattle,
you'll just split up—split up like visitors in the marketplace.
Obsessive attachment to relatives hasn't arisen for me,
which is why I severed the connection in advance.

After preserving—preserving food and wealth
   as if they were your lifeblood,
they'll just be discarded—discarded like snot.
Obsessive attachment to wealth hasn't arisen for me,
which is why I give things away to the assembly.

།གོས་ཀྱི་ལུས་རྨ་བྱ་བཞིན་དུ་སྒྲེག་སྒྲེག་ནས། །འབྲུ་ལྷོགས་བཞིན་དུ་འདོར་འདོར་འདྲ།
།བདག་གོས་ལ་ཆགས་ཞེན་མ་སྐྱེས་པས། །ད་ལྟ་བལ་ཐུལ་གྱོན་པ་དེ་ལྟར་ལགས་སོ།

།ཞེས་གཞེས་སོ།།

ཨྠི།

After decorating—decorating the body with clothes
  like a peacock,
it'll just be discarded—discarded like a snail shell.
Obsessive attachment to clothing hasn't arisen for me,
which is why I now wear coarse wool.

So he sang.

Iti

༣༥

ཙ་ཡོ་བ་རྣམས་ལ་མ་མཉེས་ཅིང་མངའ་བདག་སྟོབས་རྒྱལ་བ་ལ་སོགས་ཞལ་མ་འཛོམ་དང་འབྲལ་བ་ཐག་རིངས་ནས་བྱུང་བ་སོགས་ལ་བཞེས་པ།

།ན་མོ་གུ་རུ།

ཁ་ཆེའི་ཡུལ་ན་གུར་གུམ་སྐྱ། །ཉེ་སྐྱོ་རྒྱུད་ན་རིན་ཐང་ཆེ།

།མ་ལའི་ཡུལ་ན་ཙན་དན་ཤིང་། །ཉེ་སྐྱོ་རྒྱུད་ན་རིན་ཐང་ཆེ།

།རྒྱ་གར་ཡུལ་ན་ག་བུར་ཀྱུ། །ཉེ་སྐྱོ་རྒྱུད་ན་རིན་ཐང་ཆེ།

།ཛ་ཡབ་ཡུལ་ན་བཟང་པོ་དུག། །ཉེ་སྐྱོ་རྒྱུད་ན་རིན་ཐང་ཆེ།

།དཔལ་མཁན་པ་ཁྲོད་ན་སྤྲང་པོ་ཀོ་བྲག་པ། །ཉེ་སྐྱོ་རྒྱུད་ན་རིན་ཐང་ཆེ།

།སང་ནང་པར་འཆི་བའི་དུས་བྱུང་ན། །སྡུགས་པ་ཕྱི་ནས་བརྗོད་དེ་མཆིས།

།གློ་བུར་གྱི་རྣམ་རྟོག་སྐྱེས་ཅན། །སྐད་ཅིག་མའི་ཤེས་པ་དེ་ཡིས་བཟུང་།

།སེམས་མ་བཅོས་སོ་མའི་ངང་ལ་ཞོག །ཆོས་ཡིན་ལུགས་ཅིག་ནང་ནས་འཆར་ཏེ་འཆིས།།

ཅེས་གསུངས་སོ། །ཚོགས་གྲལ་ཅིག་དུ།

ཨིཐི།།

35

Sung when the people of Tsayo were displeased, offerings from King Tobgyel and others had arrived from far away, even though they had never met, and so forth:

Namo Guru

> Saffron root in the land of Kashmir,
> found nearby yet valued afar.
>
> Sandalwood in the land of Malaya,
> found nearby yet valued afar.
>
> Camphor water in the land of India,
> found nearby yet valued afar.
>
> Six fine herbs in the land of Cāmara,
> found nearby yet valued afar.
>
> The beggar Godrakpa in the charnel ground of splendid Khenpa,
> found nearby yet valued afar.
>
> If my moment of death comes tomorrow morning,
> you'll speak in praise of me later.
>
> When incidental thoughts arise,
> recognize the awareness of the moment.
>
> Leave the mind in an unfabricated, fresh state.
> The way things really are dawns from within.

So he spoke. This was in an assembly row.

Iti

༣༨

བླ་བྲང་གོང་དུ་ཐོ་རངས་ཅིག།

།།ན་མོ་གུ་རུ།

ལུས་མི་རྟག་སོས་ཀའི་ན་འུན་འདྲ།
།སེམས་དངོས་མེད་ནམ་མཁའ་སྟོང་པ་འདྲ།
།རྣམ་རྟོག་གྲུབ་མེད་བར་སྣང་གི་སེར་བུ་འདྲ།
།ཆོས་དེ་གསུམ་ལ་བསམ་མནོ་ཡང་ཡང་ཐོང་།

།ཅེས་བྲག་མཁར་དུ་ཟམ་པ་ལ་སྦྱོན་ནས་སྟུང་བའི་དབྱར་གསུང་དོ།

།ཨིཐི།།

The bridge below Tragar Daso

36

One dawn at the upper residence:

Namo Guru

Body impermanent like spring mist;
mind insubstantial like empty sky;
thoughts unestablished like breezes in space.
Think about these three points over and over.

Spoken when he had crossed the bridge at Trakar and become ill.

Iti

༣༥

ན་མོ་གུ་རུ།

མི་ཁྲིད་ཀྱི་ལྟད་མོ་ཇི་ལྟར་མཐོང་། །སྤྲང་བདག་གིས་གཟིགས་མོ་འདི་ལྟར་མཐོང་།

།ཧྲེན་ཁྲིད་པར་ཅན་སྐྱུ་གདུང་དཀར་རུ་ལ། །མཁའ་འགྲོ་རྒྱུད་ནས་མོས་གུས་བྱེད་ཅིང་གདའ།

།ཧྲེན་ཁྲིད་པར་ཅན་བྱང་ཆུབ་ཆེན་པོ་ལ། །མི་མ་ཡིན་ཞབས་ཏོག་བྱེད་ཅིང་གདའ།

།སྒྲོར་ལམ་བཀག་པས་རྟིག་པ་འགགས་པ་མཐོང་། །བདེན་པ་བདར་བས་དེ་ཉིད་ཐུབ་པ་མཐོང་།

།འགའ་ཞིག་གཞོན་ལ་དད་པ་སྐྱེས་པ་གདའ། །འགའ་ཞིག་ཡོད་པ་ཚོགས་སུ་བསྔོང་གིན་གདའ།
།འགའ་ཞིག་སྒྲུབ་པ་སྐྱུགས་སུ་སྤྱོད་པ་གདའ། །འགའ་ཞིག་འགྲོ་དོན་ཕྱོགས་མེད་ནུས་པ་གདའ།

།ཅེས་ལྷ་བྲང་འོག་ཏུ་དགེ་སློང་སངས་རྒྱས་དཔལ་གྱིས་ཚོགས་མཆོད་ཅིག་བྱས་པའི་དུས་སུ་བཞེས་པའོ།།

ཨི་ཐི།།

37

Namo Guru

How do you people see the show?
As a beggar, this is how I see the show.

To the exceptional shrine of the White Mausoleum
ḍākinīs are offering devotion from afar.

To the exceptional shrine of the Mahābodhi
nonhuman beings are offering service.

I saw the circumambulation path blocked by
an obstructing wall.
I saw it cleared away by the force of truth.

Some give birth to faith when young;
some give away what they have to the assembly;
some constantly sustain meditation;
some are able to benefit living beings impartially.

Sung at the lower residence when an offering to the assembly was made by the monk Sangye Bal.

Iti

༣༥

ན་མོ་གུ་རུ།

སྤྲང་པོ་མ་རྒྱས་གཞོན་ཙ་ན། །རི་ཁྲོད་དགོན་པ་འགྲིམ་ཙ་ན།
།ཞང་སྟོན་དང་སྟོག་ཆུང་སྒེལ་སྒོམ་གསུམ། །འདི་གསུམ་པོ་བོའི་བླ་མ་ལགས།

།བརྟའ་ཕག་དང་ཞི་བྱེད་ལམ་འབྲས་གསུམ། །འདི་གསུམ་པོ་བོའི་དམ་ཆོས་ལགས།

།མ་བཅོས་དང་སོ་མ་ལྷུག་པ་གསུམ། །འདི་གསུམ་པོ་བོའི་ལམ་ཁྱེར་ལགས།

།ཡོ་མ་དང་ཉང་མ་རི་ཐྲད་གསུམ། །འདི་གསུམ་པོ་བོའི་མཆོ་རྒྱུགས་ལགས།

།རི་གཡའ་རི་དང་གངས་རི་རྫ་རི་གསུམ། །དེ་སྤྲང་པོ་བདག་གི་དགོན་གནས་ཡིན།

།ཟས་ཤ་བལ་དང་སྤྱི་ལོ་སྣ་ལོ་གསུམ། །དེ་སྤྲང་པོ་བདག་གིས་གསོལ་ཟས་ཡིན།

།ཆུ་གཡའ་ཆུ་དང་གངས་ཆུ་རྫ་ཆུ་གསུམ། །དེ་སྤྲང་པོ་བདག་གི་བཏུང་ཆུ་ཡིན།

།ཤ་བ་དང་རྐྱ་བ་རྣ་བ་གསུམ། །དེ་སྤྲང་པོ་བདག་གི་གྲོགས་ཕྱུགས་ལགས།

།བྱ་གོང་མོ་དང་ཐི་བྱ་སྲེག་པ་གསུམ། །དེ་སྤྲང་པོ་བདག་གིས་ཁྱིམ་ཚེས་ཡིན།

།སེམས་ཀྱི་སེམས་ལ་བལྟ་བ་དེ། །དེ་སྤྲང་པོ་བདག་གི་ཉམས་ལེན་ཡིན།

38

Namo Guru

When this beggar wasn't old, but young,
wandering in isolated mountain ranges,
Zhangdön, Ngogchung, and Nyelgom,
these three were my masters.

Hayagrīva with Vārāhī, Pacification, and the Path with the Result,
these three were my excellent Dharma.

Being unfabricated, fresh, and relaxed,
these three were my constant path.

Leaves, turnips, and mountain grass,
these three were my provisions.

Slate mountains, glacial mountains, and clay mountains,
these three were this beggar's secluded places.

Mushrooms, sedum, and knotweed for food,
these three were this beggar's sustenance.

Water from slate streams, glacial streams, and clay streams,
these three were this beggar's drinking water.

Deer, antelope, and argali,
these three were this beggar's livestock.

White grouse, pigeons, and partridges,
these three were this beggar's neighbors.

Mind watching mind,
that's this beggar's experience of practice.

།བདག་པས་གཞན་གཅེས་བྱེད་པ་དེ། །དེ་སྤྲང་པོ་བདག་གི་ལག་ལན་ཡིན།

།བདག་ལ་དད་ཅིང་གུས་པ་རྣམས། །སྤྲང་བདག་བཞིན་བྱས་ན་སྐྱིད་པར་མཆི།

ཨིཐི༎

Cherishing others more than myself,
that's this beggar's application of practice.

Those who are faithful and devoted to me,
if you act like this beggar, you'll be happy.

Iti

༣༨

ན་མོ་གུ་རུ།

ཕྱིའི་ནམ་མཁའ་དངོས་པོ་དང་མཚན་མས་སྟོང༌། །ནང་གི་སེམས་ཉིད་དངོས་པོ་དང་མཚན་མས་སྟོང་ངོ།

།དངོས་མེད་ཀྱི་ནམ་མཁའ་སྣང་རྒྱུ་ཅིར་ཡང་སྣང་ངོ། །དངོས་མེད་ཀྱི་སེམས་ཉིད་མ་འགགས་པ་ནི་ཅིར་ཡང་སྣང་ངོ།

།ནམ་མཁའ་དང་སེམས་ཉིད་མགོ་སྙོམས་པ་ཡིན་གསུང་ངོ།

ཨིཐཱི།།

39

Namo Guru

External sky empty of substantiality and characteristic;
internal nature of mind empty of substantiality and characteristic.

The way the insubstantial sky appears is that it may
appear as anything.
The ceaseless insubstantial nature of mind may also
appear as anything.

A statement that the sky and the nature of mind are comparable.

Iti

༨༠

།ན་མོ་གུ་རུ།

ཨོཾ་མ་ཎི་པདྨེ་ཧཱུྃ།

།ད་ལོའི་ལོ་འདི་ཅིའི་ལོ། །ད་ལོའི་ལོ་འདི་འབྲུག་གི་ལོ།

།འབྲུག་སྒྲ་ཅན་གཡུ་འབྲུག་སྔོན་མོ་ལ། །མཁན་པ་ཁྲོད་ཀྱི་རི་རྩེ་ལ།
།རྣམ་པར་རྒྱལ་མའི་ཁང་བཟངས་རྩིགས། །ཀུན་དང་པ་འདྲེན་པའི་ཁྲིམ་ཅིག་བྱུང་།

།བླ་མའི་ཞལ་ནས་དེ་སྐད་ཟེར་རོ་གྲིས་ལ་རྒྱུད་དུ་སྦྲོགས།།

40

Namo Guru

Oṃ Maṇi Padme Hūṃ

Now what year is the year this year?
The year this year is a dragon year.

In the year of the thunderous blue turquoise dragon,
on the mountain peak of Khenpa charnel ground,
a fine Vijayā temple has been built,
a house that elicits faith in everyone.

Announce afar that this was spoken by the master.

༨༡

ན་མོ་གུ་རུ།

གནས་ཡངས་པ་ཅན་གྱི་དིང་རི་དེ། །གནས་ཕུལ་དུ་ཕྱིན་པའི་བླ་འབོར་དེ།

།ནུབ་ཀྱི་རི་ནི་སྐྱོབ་པ་འདྲ། །ཤར་གྱི་ལྷུངས་ནི་བཞོལ་བ་འདྲ།
།བྱང་གི་རི་ནི་སྐྱོར་བ་འདྲ། །ལྷོའི་ཐང་ནི་བཏིང་བ་འདྲ།
།ཆབ་རྒྱུན་ཆད་མེད་ཅིག་མདུན་ན་འབབ།

།བྲ་ཀ་ལ་འདའ་ཀ་གནས་པ་ཡི། །དེ་ལྟ་བུའི་གནས་མཆོག་དེ།
།རྗེ་རྒྱ་གར་གྱི་རིང་ལ་བཟུང་ནས་གདའ། །གྲུབ་ཐོབ་གོང་མའི་རིང་ལ་བཞུགས་ནས་གདའ།
།སྤྲང་བདག་གིས་རིང་ལ་འཁོར་འཁོར་འདྲ།

།ཧོར་ནག་པོ་ལྷག་རུས་བར་དུ་གཉེམ།

།བླ་མ་དཀོན་མཆོག་མེད་དམ་ཐུགས་རྗེས་ཟུང་།

།ཡི་དམ་ལྷ་ཚོགས་མེད་དམ་བྱིན་གྱིས་བརླབས།

།ཆོས་སྐྱོང་བསྲུངས་མ་མེད་དམ་དམག་སྣ་ཟློག

།སླུ་དགའ་ནས་མ་བླངས་སྐྱོ་ནས་བླངས།
།ཚིག་སྙན་ནས་མ་སྒྲིགས་ཤུགས་ལ་བྱུང་།

།ཧོར་འུད་བྱུང་དུས་བྲག་མདའ་སྒྲོར་བཞེས་སོ།

41

Namo Guru

That spacious site of Tingri,
that marvelous site of Langkor.

Western mountains like a rampart;
eastern valley like a slope;
northern mountains like a cluster;
southern plain like a floor;
river constantly flooding in front.

Such a sublime site as that, where the nightingale lives,
was taken during the time of the Indian Lord,
was a residence during the time of former adepts,
and may be lost—lost during this beggar's time.

The evil Mongols have hit the backs of our skulls.

Are there no master and Three Jewels?
Hold us with compassion.

Is there no assembly of divine chosen deities?
Grant your blessings.

Are there no guardian Dharma protectors?
Repel the army.

I don't sing from joy; I sing from sorrow.
This won't be fixed with pleasant words,
it will happen naturally.

Sung at Trakdadro when the Mongols swept in.

༨༢

།ན་མོ་གུ་རུ།

གནམ་ལ་གཟའ་སྐར་དྲངས་མང་ཡང་། །གཟའ་ཉི་མའི་སྙིང་པོའི་གོང་ན་མེད།

།ས་ལ་འབབ་ཆུ་དྲངས་མང་ཡང་། །ཆུ་རྒྱུན་ཆད་མེད་པ་གཱ་གཱའི་ཆུ།

།རྩི་ཤིང་དང་ནགས་ཚལ་དྲངས་མང་ཡང་། །ཤིང་ཙན་དན་སྡོང་པོའི་གོང་ན་མེད།

།དབུས་བཙང་ན་བུ་སློབ་དྲངས་མང་ཡང་། །དམ་ཚིག་དག་པ་དོ་ཉུབ་ཙམ།

།ཡང་དག་ཟབ་དོན་དྲངས་མང་ཡང་། །ཐབས་ཤེས་རབ་ཀྱི་གོང་ན་ཅིག་དང་མེད།

།ཅེས་ཉ་མ་ཁ་ཅིག་གི་ཚོགས་མཆོད་ཅིག་བྱས་དུས་བཞེས་སོ།།

ཨྠི།།

42

Namo Guru

Numerous planets and stars in the sky,
but no planet superior to the heart of the sun.

Numerous rivers flowing on the earth,
but the ceaseless river is the river Gangā.

Numerous fruit trees and forest groves,
but no tree superior to the sandal tree.

Numerous close disciples in Ü and Tsang,
but the sacred commitments are pure just tonight.

Numerous perfectly profound truths,
but none superior to method and transcendent knowledge.

Sung when an offering to the assembly was made by several female disciples.

Iti

༨༣

རྨི་ལམ་དུ་ནམ་སྐྱོད་ཇོ་མོ་གཉིས་ཙམ་སྤྲ་དུམ་དུ་གཤེགས་སུ་མི་ཡོང་ཟེར་ཏེ་ཡལ་སོང་། དེ་ནས་ཡང་དར་ཅིག་ན་མི་ཁ་ཅིག་དང་བླ་མ་རི་ཁ་ཅིག་ན་འདུག་པས། ཁོ་པ་ན་རེ་ཁྱི་ར་བྱེད་པའི་སྤྱོད་འདྲ་འུ་འདི་ཏུ་ཅེད་པ་ཟེར་བ་ལ་རྨི་ལམ་དུ་བཞེས་པ།

ན་མོ་གུ་རུ།

བཙང་ཕྲུ་ཐུམ་གྱི་ལམ་ཁར། ཆག་གི་སྐྱུ་སྐྱུར་མགུར་འདི་བཞེས་པ།

།སྤྱོད་ཉིད་ཀྱི་ཐང་ཀ་ཡངས་མོ་ལ། །རྣམ་རྟོག་གི་རི་དགས་ཤ་གཡག་རྒྱུས།

།ཁྱི་རྟ་གཉིས་ཀྱི་གཞའ་བཅག་ནས། །གྲི་མདའ་གཉིས་ཀྱི་བཞུག་རྟུལ་ནས།
།རྣམ་རྟོག་གི་རི་དགས་ཤ་གཡག་གསད།

།ཤ་ནི་གཉིས་སུ་མེད་པར་ཟོས། །རོ་ནི་བདེ་བ་ཆེན་པོར་སྨྱོང་།

།བདག་ཁྱི་ར་བྱེད་ན་དེ་ལྟར་བྱེད།

།ཅེས་གསུངས་སོ།།

ཨིཐི།།

43

In a dream two ladies said early one evening, "He won't come to Dradum in Tsang," and vanished. Then for a moment several people and the master were on the face of a mountain. They said, "Let's do our hunting here," and he sang in the dream.

Namo Guru

He sang this song at Chagi Gyagya on the road to Dradum in Tsang:

> On the vast plain of emptiness
> the wild beasts and bull yaks of thought circulate.
>
> Breaking their pride with both dog and horse,
> subduing them with both sword and spear,
> I kill the wild beasts and bull yaks of thought.
>
> The flesh is eaten in nonduality,
> the taste experienced as great bliss.
>
> If I go hunting, that's how I do it.

So he spoke.

Iti

༨༨

ན་མོ་གུ་རུ།

པྲ་དུམ་ནས་མར་བྱོན་པའི་ལམ་ཁར། ཤོ་རྗེ་ཨག་ཚལ་གྱི་འགྲམ་དུ་བཞེས་པ།

རྗེ་དྲིན་ཅན་གྱི་བླ་མ་རིན་པོ་ཆེ། །མི་འབྲལ་སྤྱི་གཙུག་བརྒྱན་དུ་བཞུགས།
།བཞུགས་ནས་བྱིན་གྱིས་བརླབ་ཏུ་གསོལ།

།བལྟ་བ་སྣང་སྲིད་ཀྱི་གཞི་བཞེངས་འདི་ལ། །བལྟ་བ་ལོག་གིས་དོགས་པའི་དུ་ཁ་བཀྲིས་པས།
།སྒོམ་པ་ཐམས་ཅད་འཆིང་བར་གདའ་བས།

།སྐལ་ལྡན་ཀུན་སེམས་སྒོམ་པས་མ་འཆིང་ཡན་པར་ཐོང་ལ། །དོན་ཡན་པའི་སྟེང་ནས་གཟིགས་མོ་མཛོད།

།བསྒོམ་པ་མཚན་མ་རང་གྲོལ་འདི། །བསྒོམ་གོལ་གྱིས་དོགས་པའི་དུ་ཁ་དཀྲིས་པས།
།སྒོམ་པ་ཐམས་ཅད་འཆིང་བར་གདའ་བས།

།སྐལ་ལྡན་ཀུན་སེམས་སྒོམ་པས་མ་འཆིང་ཡན་པར་ཐོང་ལ། །དོན་ཡན་པའི་སྟེང་ནས་གཟིགས་མོ་མཛོད།

།སྤྱོད་པ་ཤུགས་འབྱུང་འགག་མེད་འདི། །སྤྱོད་པ་རྩིངས་ཀྱིས་དོགས་པའི་དུ་ཁ་དཀྲིས་པས།
།སྒོམ་པ་ཐམས་ཅད་འཆིང་བར་གདའ་བས།

།སྐལ་ལྡན་ཀུན་སེམས་སྒོམ་པས་མ་འཆིང་ཡན་པར་ཐོང་ལ། །དོན་ཡན་པའི་སྟེང་ནས་གཟིགས་མོ་མཛོད།

44

Namo Guru

On the road coming back from Dradum he sang beside the grove of Shodo Ak.

Precious lord and kind master,
always present as a crown ornament on my head,
dwelling here, please grant your blessing.

This basic ground of apparent existence is the view,
but perverted view creates the suffering of doubt,
and all meditation becomes binding.

All who are fortunate, set yourselves free
  with the mind unbound by meditation,
and observe reality from a state of freedom.

This natural liberation of conceptual marks is the meditation,
but wrong meditation creates the suffering of doubt,
and all meditation becomes binding.

All who are fortunate, set yourselves free
  with the mind unbound by meditation,
and observe reality from a state of freedom.

This unimpeded, relaxed state is the conduct,
but coarse conduct creates the suffering of doubt,
and all meditation becomes binding.

All who are fortunate, set yourselves free
  with the mind unbound by meditation,
and observe reality from a state of freedom.

།འབྲས་བུ་སྐུ་གསུམ་དབྱེར་མེད་འདི། །འབྲས་བུ་མ་ཐོབ་ཀྱི་དོགས་པའི་དུ་ཁ་དཀྲིས་པས།
།སྒྲོམ་པ་ཐམས་ཅད་འཆིང་བར་གདའ་བས།

།སྐལ་ལྡན་ཀུན་སེམས་སྒྲོམ་པས་མ་འཆིང་ཡན་པར་ཐོང་ལ། །དོན་ཡན་པའི་སྙིང་ནས་གཟིགས་མོ་མཛོད།

།ང་ནམ་མཁའ་ལྟ་བུའི་རྣལ་འབྱོར་པ། །ནམ་མཁའི་མཚན་ཉིད་མི་རྟོགས་ཀྱི།
།ཁྲིད་མ་གོ་བ་ཚོ་སྐུར་པ་མ་འདེབས་མཛོད།

།ང་ནོར་བུ་ལྟ་བུའི་རྣལ་འབྱོར་པ། །གསོལ་བ་བཏབ་ན་དགོས་འདོད་འབྱུང་།
།མོས་གུས་གྱིས་ཅིག་བུ་སློབ་ཀུན།།

།ཨྠི།།

This indivisibility of the three buddha bodies is the result,
but not achieving the result creates the suffering of doubt,
and all meditation becomes binding.

All who are fortunate, set yourselves free
with the mind unbound by meditation,
and observe reality from a state of freedom.

I'm a yogi like the sky.
You who don't understand, having not realized
the characteristic of the sky—don't condemn me!

I'm a yogi like a wish-fulfilling gem.
If you supplicate me, needs and desires will be fulfilled.
All you close disciples—have devotion!

Iti

ཨེ་མ་ཧོ།

སྲིད་གསུམ་འདྲན་བྲལ་གྲུབ་ཐོབ་ཀྱི་བྲག་པས། །མགུར་འབུམ་སྙན་ངག་བློས་བྱས་ཚིག་དང་བྲལ།
།གཉུག་མ་བློ་འདས་རང་འབྱུང་འགག་མེད་ཤར།

།ཤུགས་འབྱུང་རང་རྩོལ་འབོལ་རྩོམ་ལྷུག་པ་འདི། །རོ་ཅིག་དུ་མའི་གསུང་དུ་ཤར་བ་རྣམས།
།ཡ་མཚན་སྨད་བྱུང་ཞིན་དུ་ཟབ་མཐོང་ནས། །ལྷ་བཙུན་རིན་རྣམས་བདག་གིས་པར་དུ་སྒྲུབས།

།འདི་བྲིས་དགེ་བས་འགྲོ་དྲུག་སེམས་ཅན་རྣམས། །གྲུབ་ཐོབ་དེ་མཉམ་རྟོགས་པ་མངོན་གྱུར་ནས།
།གཉུག་མ་ལྷན་ཅིག་སྐྱེས་པ་མངོན་གྱུར་ཏེ། །རྒྱུད་དྲུག་སེམས་ཅན་སྨིན་གྲོལ་འགོད་པར་ཤོག །

ཨེ་ཝཾ།།

འདི་ཡན་དགེ་འདུན་ཆོས།

བཀྲ་ཤིས།

Woodblocks for printing books at Tragar Daso

[Colophon]

E Ma Ho

The poetry in the collected songs of the adept Godrakpa,
who is peerless in the three worlds,
is free from mentally fabricated phrases, and dawned
  in a primordial, transcendent, self-arisen,
    unimpeded way.

I, Lhatsun Rin Nam, saw that these casual, relaxed,
self-emergent, free compositions,
in which a single taste dawns in various words,
were marvelous, wonderful, and very profound,
and had them printed.

By the virtue of writing this, may the sentient beings
  of the six realms actualize realization
    equal to that of this adept,
and actualizing the coemergent primordial state,
  may the six types of sentient beings be established
    in maturation and liberation.

Evaṃ

(The preceeding was carved by Gendun.)

Good fortune!

Notes to the Translation

Godrakpa *(Ko rag pa):* On the title page, and at several points in the text, the spelling *ko rag* is found instead of the usual *ko brag.* This spelling may reflect the pronunciation in the region of Tibet where the text was originally published.

three realms *(khams gsum):* the desire realm *('dod khams),* form realm *(gzugs khams),* and formless realm *(gzugs med khams).*

Vajra Dhvaja *(badzra dho dza):* Sanskrit for "Vajra Banner," which is Dorje Gyaltsen *(Rdo rje rgyal mtshan)* in Tibetan. The same words are also found on the title pages of other works published at Tragar Daso by Lhatsun Rinchen Namgyel. The significance of the words here is uncertain. Perhaps they are a Sanskrit rendering of the Tibetan name Dorje Gyaltsen, which may have been the name of someone connected with the publing projects, such as a patron.

Namo Guru Deva Ḍākinī *(na mo gu ru de wa ḍa ki ni):* Sanskrit for "Homage to the master, deity, and ḍākinī." This initial expression of homage by the editor, Lhatsun Rinchen Namgyel, is also found in the beginning of his edition of the collected songs of Marpa Lotsawa.

buddha body of form *(gzugs sku):* The buddha body of form is composed of the emanation buddha body *(nirmāṇakāya, sprul pa'i sku)* and the buddha body of rapture *(sambhogakāya, longs spyod rdzogs pa'i sku).*

1

Namo Ratna Guru *(na mo radṇa gu ru):* Sanskrit for "Homage to the precious master."

Segyu *(Sad kyu):* This may be a corruption of the name Sakya *(Sa skya).* Superfluous vowel signs are also found elsewhere in the text. The great monastery of Sakya was the most important Tibetan center of higher learning during Godrakpa's lifetime.

the teacher Dong: According to Shes rab mgon, *Chos,* 2a, while still a young boy Godrakpa received teachings on some grammatical treatises from a teacher named Dengtrak *(Ldeng grags),* which is probably a variant spelling for Dongtrak *(Ldong grags).*

The Weapon to Open the Door of Speech (Smra sgo mtshon cha): This text was written by the Indian master Smṛtijñāna while he lived in Tibet in the tenth and eleventh centuries. It is one of the earliest and most important Tibetan grammatical treatises. According to Shākya mchog ldan, *Smra,* 291–92, Smṛtijñāna wrote the text in Sanskrit and translated it into Tibetan himself.

Langkor *(Bla 'khor):* The hermitage of Langkor *(Glang 'khor)* in Tingri *(Ding ri)* near the Tibetan border with Nepal was founded in 1097 by the Indian master Phadampa Sangye (*Pha dam pa Sangs rgyas,* d. 1105) and was his main residence in Tibet.

the teacher and master: When Godrakpa was fifteen years old, he first met the master Dorje Bal of Gyamrim *(Rgyam rim Rdo rje dpal).* See Shes rab mgon, *Chos,* 2a–b.

Amoghapāśa *(Don yod zhags pa):* This tantric deity is a peaceful form of the bodhisattva Avalokiteśvara, the divine embodiment of compassion.

Vajrapāṇi *(Phyag na rdo rje):* This tantric deity is the wrathful divine embodiment of enlightened energy and power.

Nyanang *(Snya nang):* region near the Tibetan border with Nepal, not far from Godrakpa's birthplace of Tingri.

the gate of the excellent Dharma: At eighteen years of age, Godrakpa took the Buddhist vows of a lay novice from the master Semikpa *(Se mig pa),* who would become one of his most important teachers. At this time, he also received a number of significant Dharma teachings from this master, including the instructions of the Path with the Result in the tradition of Lady Machik Zhama. See Shes rab mgon, *Chos,* 2a–b.

agitated states of mind *(blo sbram):* an obscure term. Tulku Sangak Rinpoche was uncertain of the meaning, but suggested *rgod po,* which means "wild" or "agitated."

Zhangdön *(Zhang ston):* another name for the master Semikpa. See Ngor chen, *Lam,* 116.2, who refers to Zhangdön Semikpa *(Zhang ston Se mig pa)* and states that Godrakpa received from him the teachings of the Path with the Result in the tradition of Lady Machik Zhama. Also see Shes rab mgon, *Chos,* 2a–b, for a list of teachings Godrakpa received from Semikpa.

the complete four initiations: The four tantric initiations are the vase initiation, the secret initiation, the initiation of transcendent knowledge dependent on an embodiment of primordial awareness, and the fourth initiation. This is probably a reference to the teachings of the Path with the Result, the practice of which is intimately linked to the four initiations.

taking refuge and awakening the enlightenment mind: The most basic vow in Buddhism is that of taking refuge in the Three Jewels, which are the Buddha, the Dharma, and the Saṅgha. In the tradition of the Mahāyāna, or Great Vehicle, one also cultivates the aspiration to attain complete enlightenment for the sake of all living beings. This is referred to as "awakening the enlightenment mind."

the mother tantras of secret mantra: In the tradition of secret mantra, or the Vajrayāna, there is often a threefold classification of the highest tantras. The mother tantras are those that emphasize primordial awareness, the father tantras are those that emphasize skillful method, and the nondual tantras are those that give equal weight to both primordial awareness and skillful method.

Stages of the Path: The instructions of the Stages of the Path *(Lam rim)* according to the Gadam *(Bka' gdams)* tradition were largely founded on teachings brought to Tibet by the Indian master Atiśa (c. 982–1054) in the middle of the eleventh century.

Perfections: In general, the Perfections according to the tradition of the Mahāyāna, or Great Vehicle, are the Six Perfections of generosity, moral discipline, patience, diligence, meditation, and transcendent knowledge.

Great Seal *(Phyag rgya chen po):* a term used to designate a genre of teachings on the nature of the mind, as well as a term for the result achieved through tantric practices. Teachings of the Great Seal are found in all the Tibetan traditions, but the various Kagyu *(Bka' brgyud)* lineages specialize in them.

Acalanātha *(Mi g.yo mgon po):* The tantric deity Acalanātha is a wrathful manifestation of the bodhisattva Mañjuśrī, the divine embodiment of primordial awareness.

three topics of Abhidharma: The Abhidharma is a corpus of Indian Buddhist teachings on cosmology and psychology. The three topics *(gnas gsum)* are unidentified.

Great Middle Way *(Dbu ma chen po):* a term used for a specific lineage of the philosophical teachings of the Madhyamaka, or Middle Way, in which elements from the Cittamātra, or Mind Only, tradition of Indian Buddhist philosophy are incorporated.

So's Naked Perception of Intrinsic Awareness (Bso'i rig pa cer mthong): According to the biography of Godrakpa's disciple Chim Namka Trak (*Mchims Nam mkha' grags,* 1210–85), who was the throne-holder of the important Gadam *(Bka' gdams)* monastery of Nartang *(Snar thang)* from 1250 to 1258, this teaching is from the Pacification *(Zhi byed)* tradition of Phadampa Sangye. See Smon lam tshul khrims, *Mchims,* 13b. I am grateful to Per Sorensen for a copy of this work. So Chungpa (*So chung pa,* 1062–1128) was an important disciple of Phadampa through whom one of the main lineages of the Pacification teachings was transmitted. See Roerich (1976), 876–81.

The Dohā Trilogy (Mdo' ha skor gsum): a set of three texts on the teachings of the Great Seal composed by the Indian adept Saraha. All three have recently been translated and studied in Guenther (1993).

the teacher and master of Langkor: the teacher Dorje Bal of Gyamrim, from whom Godrakpa had earlier received lay vows and teachings. See Shes rab mgon, *Chos,* 2b.

The Tenth Upholder of Intrinsic Awareness (Rig 'dzin bcu pa): unidentified. Possibly this was an otherwise unknown aural transmission unique to Godrakpa's teacher Dorje Bal. Roerich (1976), 726, states that this is the name of a Nyingma *(Rnying ma)* text.

The Finger Pointed at the Old Woman (Rgan mo 'dzub tshugs): a brief instruction pointing out the true nature of the mind according to the Great Perfection *(Rdzogs chen).* The teaching was given by Guru Padmasambhava to a devoted old woman who had been serving him yogurt every morning. See Padmasambhava, *Rgan.*

Great Perfection *(Rdzogs chen):* a special genre of instructions specific to the Nyingma *(Rnying ma)* tradition of Tibetan Buddhism.

Josey of Gyaphub *(Rgya phubs Jo sras):* This name is given as Josey of Gyaphuk *(Rgya phug gyi jo sras)* in Shes rab mgon, *Chos,* 2b.

The Heart Sūtra: This is the popular condensed version of the voluminous scriptures of the *Prajñāpāramitā,* or *The Perfection of Transcendent Knowledge.*

Nyödön *(Gnyos ston):* The name is given as Nyöndön *(Snyon ston)* in Shes rab mgon, *Chos,* 2b.

Nyelgom *(Snyal sgom):* The name is given as Nyengom *(Snyen sgom)* in Shes rab mgon, *Chos,* 2b.

Cutting the Stream *(Rgyun gcod):* The profound instructions of The Great Seal for Cutting the Stream of Saṃsāra *(Phyag rgya chen po 'khor ba rgyun gcod)* were first taught by the ḍākinīs of Uḍḍiyana to the Indian adept Saraha, who then granted them to Mitrayogin. Mitrayogin came to Tibet and taught them to Lady Machik Sangye Rema *(Ma gcig Sangs rgyas re ma)*. See Roerich (1976), 1039–41.

Nakpo Tsita *(Nag po tsi ta):* unidentified.

Kharak Tsangpa *(Kha rag Gtsang pa):* another name for Nyö Chögyi Ziji *(Gnyos Chos kyi gzi brjid)* of Kharak *(Kha rag)*. See note 26 to the introduction.

The Path with the Result *(Lam 'bras):* a vast system of tantric theory and meditation techniques based on the brief *Vajra Verses (Rdo rje tshig rkang)* of the Indian adept Virūpa. These teachings were first bestowed on Virūpa by Vajra Nairātmyā, the consort of the tantric deity Hevajra.

Shertsul the teacher of Mönkhar: Godrakpa also received the teachings of the Path with the Result in the tradition of Lady Machik Zhama from Shertsul *(Sher tshul)* of Mönkhar *(Smon mkhar)*. This master's full name was Sherab Tsultrim *(Shes rab tshul 'khrims)*. He was a nephew of Zhama *(Zhwa ma'i dbon po)* and was also known as Josey of Mönkhar *(Smon mkhar Jo sras)*. See Ngor chen, *Lam*, 116.2.

E Ma Ho *(e ma ho):* an expression of wonder.

Siddhi Phala Ho *(si hi pha la ho):* a Sanskrit phrase expressing wonder *(ho)* at the result *(phala)* of attainment *(siddhi)*. A similar phrase is found at the beginning of song 22.

Iti *(ithi):* "The End." A Sanskrit particle used at the end of chapters and sections of books.

2

Drok Labchi *('Brog La phyi):* an area north of Mt. Everest near the Tibetan border with Nepal. It is most well known as a region where the great yogin Milarepa spent much time in meditation. According to Shes rab mgon, *Chos*, 3b, the experiences described in this song occurred while Godrakpa was meditating at a place called Senge Trak *(Seng ge brag)* in Labchi. Song 10 was also sung at this site.

experiential appearances *(nyams kyi snang ba):* a fundamental term in the teachings of the Path with the Result. The entire instructions of this tradition may be explained in the context of what are known as "the three appearances" *(snang* *gsum).* These are the three ways phenomena appear to an ordinary sentient being, a yoga practitioner, and a buddha, respectively. In the broadest sense, the term "experiential appearances" is used to describe everything that appears to a yoga practitioner in whose mindstream at least one experience of meditative concentration has arisen. Godrakpa's surviving commentary on the Path with the Result is almost solely devoted to explaining the phenomena of the "experiential appearances." See Ko brag pa, *Lam,* 452–585.

gathering of the constituents *(khams 'dus pa):* In the teachings of the Path with the Result, there are three "gatherings of the constituents." These are three stages on the path, during which "the constituents" of the vital winds and the clear essences of the physical constituents are "gathered" into specific locations in the subtle channels as a result of certain yoga practices. Definitions of all three gatherings using almost precisely the same words as in this song are given in Ko brag pa, *Lam,* 579–81. The wording used in this song and Godrakpa's treatise on the Path with the Result is somewhat different than in other extant works on the same topic.

depression *(snying rlung):* literally "wind in the heart"—a term used in Tibetan medicine for a respiratory illness that produces symptoms of groundless depression and anxiety.

the first gathering of the constituents: The process of the first gathering of the constituents is likened to the harsh winter wind. During this period the vital winds *(rlung)* are harmful; there is discomfort and pain of the vital winds and subtle channels *(rtsa)* of the body; and the mind comes to rest only with difficulty. See Ko brag pa, *Lam,* 579–80.

This appearance of the objects of the six groups, as for an elephant crazed with beer, was seething, shimmering, turbulent: Almost identical lines occur in a song about the Path with the Result written by Godrakpa's disciple Yangönpa. See Yang dgon pa, *Rgyal,* 210: *phyi yul gyi snang ba sna tshogs 'di/ glang chen chang gis smyos pa bzhin/ bu ne long nge zing nge 'dug//.* The six groups are the apparently external objects of the six groups of the consciousnesses: sight, hearing, smell, taste, body, and mind.

the middle gathering of the constituents: The process of the middle gathering of the constituents is likened to the wind in springtime, which is reduced in harshness. During this period the vital winds are neither harmful nor beneficial, there is pain of the drops *(thig le),* and there is a stabilizing of visionary appearances *(mthong snang).* See Ko brag pa, *Lam,* 579–80.

Māra *(Bdud):* the name of the Buddha's demonic tempter and a class of demonic forces.

love and affection forsaken: Godrakpa has just left behind all those who have been expressing their love and affection for him through offerings and praises, which he recognizes as potential obstacles.

Others saw me buy suffering with happiness: Other people did not understand how Godrakpa could give up a comfortable and happy situation for the hard life of a roaming beggar yogin.

the final gathering of the constituents: Godrakpa likens the final gathering of the constituents to a soothing, gentle breeze. (The spelling *bse ru* in the song should be corrected to *ser bu.* See Ko brag pa, *Lam,* 580.) At this point the vital winds are beneficial and produce good qualities. There is also realization of the six subsequent mindfulnesses: the master, the Buddha, the Dharma, the Saṅgha, moral discipline, and generosity. One is now able to see some emanation buddha bodies *(nirmāṇa-kāya).* See Ko brag pa, *Lam,* 579–80.

3

like little birds in the top of a tree: an example traditionally used for things that will not remain very long. This song about the Six Perfections (generosity, moral discipline, patience, diligence, meditation, and transcendent knowledge) is a very close rendering of an earlier song by Jetsun Milarepa. See Rus pa'i rgyan can (= Gtsang smyon He ru ka), *Rnal,* 272, and Chang (1962), vol. 1, 100.

freedoms and endowments *(dal 'byor):* That which is traditionally referred to in Buddhism as a "precious human existence" is composed of eighteen "freedoms and endowments." The eight freedoms are freedom from birth as a hell being, a hungry ghost, an animal, a god, a barbarian, one with perverse view, one living in an age when there is no buddha, and one who is mute. The first five endowments refer to oneself and are to be born as a human being, to be born in a central land, to have complete sense faculties, to have faith in the Dharma, and not to commit the worst crimes. The second five endowments refer to others and are for a buddha to appear, for that buddha to teach the Dharma, for the Dharma to endure, for there to be followers, and for there to be compassion for others.

4

fraud *(srang can):* an obscure term. Tulku Sangak Rinpoche suggested the possible synonym of *g.yo sgyu can,* and recalled seeing the term *mi rgod srang can* in other old texts.

home *(pha yul):* literally "fatherland." I have chosen to translate this term throughout the songs as "home" because of Godrakpa's emphasis on the renunciation of a secular life, not just familiar surroundings.

In place of demons, I'm afflicted by the master's oral instructions; in place of demonesses, I'm blessed by ḍākinīs. The Great Seal supports me from behind: These three lines are from a song by Milarepa. In the popular version of his songs, they are found in a song he sung when meeting Phadampa Sangye. See Chang (1962), vol. 2, 611, who interprets the lines somewhat differently.

depression *(snying rlung):* See note to song 2.

ghost *(srog yol):* an obscure term. According to Tulku Sangak Rinpoche, it is sometimes seen as a term for a corpse *(ro)* or a deceased person *(gshin po).*

five poisons: The five poisons are desire or attachment, hatred or aversion, ignorance, pride, and jealousy.

lancet *(zu gu):* an obscure term. Tulku Sangak Rinpoche explained it as a thin sharp instrument used to lance and drain boils and other infections.

Nyanam *(Snya nam):* a variant spelling for Nyanang (Snya nang). See note to song 1.

Vajradhara *(Rdo rje 'chang):* a name for the divine form of the buddha body of reality, and the ultimate source of the tantric teachings.

5

three dynamic states *(rtsal gsum):* unidentified.

honored on the heads of all: In tantric meditations the teacher is often visualized on the crown of one's head.

three buddha bodies *(sku gsum):* The three buddha bodies are the buddha body of reality *(dharmakāya, chos sku),* the buddha body of rapture *(sambhogakāya, longs spyod rdzogs pa'i sku),* and the emanation buddha body *(nirmāṇakāya, sprul sku).*

6

Kyurgar on Mt. Tsi *(Rtswi ri Khyur skar):* The spelling is given in the biography as Kungar on Mt. Shrī *(Shrī ri Khung dkar).* See Shes rab mgon, *Chos,* 4b, where the spelling is consistently Shrī ri in all instances. In many other sources the spelling is Rtsib ri. This is a range of mountains on the northwest perimeter of the Tingri plain.

Mt. Tsi of the Victors in Ladö: The term Ladö *(La stod)* is used for a large area of west Tibet in the district of Tsang *(Gtsang).* Mt. Tsi of the Victors *(Rgyal gyi rtsi ri),* which is also referred to as Mt. Shrī *(Shrī ri)* or Mt. Tsib *(Rtsib ri),* was a favorite early site for meditation, especially in the Kagyu *(Bka' brgyud)* lineages. For example, Marpa Lotsawa told his disciple Milarepa to meditate there because it had been blessed by great Indian adepts. See Lhalungpa (1977), 94.

The Recitation of the Names of Mañjuśrī ('Jam dpal mtshan brjod): The *Mañjuśrī-nāmasaṃgīti* is one of the most authoritative tantric scriptures. It has been studied and translated in Davidson (1981).

The Praise of the Names of the Sugata (Bde bshegs mtshan bstod): This text may perhaps be identified as the *Tathāgata nāmasaṃgīti kalpikabhadrālaṃkāra māla (Bde bshin gshegs pa'i mtshan brjod bskal bzang rgyan gyi phreng ba),* written by the Indian master Jinaputra. It is found in the Peking edition of the Tibetan Tripiṭaka, vol. 46: 115.2.1–117.5.2.

The Three Things of Wealth ('Byor pa'i rdzas gsum): unidentified.

the Great Brahmin: the renowned Indian adept Saraha.

The Dohā Trilogy (Do ha skor gsum): Saraha's three most important songs expressing the realization of the Great Seal.

the external objects of the six groups: the apparently external objects of the six groups of the consciousnesses: sight, hearing, smell, taste, body, and mind.

Tumbu man: The term Tumbu *(Dum bu)* is used to designate Godrakpa's racial stock *(mi'i rigs).* Godrakpa's paternal clan *(gdung)* name was Dong *(Ldong).* See Shes rab mgon, *Chos,* 1b. 'Jam mgon Kong sprul, *Theg,* vol. 1, 523, also refers to Godrakpa as Dum bu Ko brag pa, as does 'Jam mgon A mes zhabs, *Yongs,* 173, and other authors.

the three vows: The three vows are the vow of individual liberation according to the Hinayāna, the bodhisattva vow according to the Mahāyāna, and the tantric vows of the Vajrayāna.

two hundred and fifty rules: a rough reference to the 253 rules governing the conduct of fully ordained monks according to the monastic code of the Vinaya.

7

Khenpa charnel ground *(Mkhan pa khrod):* Godrakpa often lived at the Khenpa charnel ground to the west of Langkor in Tingri. This place had also been the principal residence of the Indian master Phadampa Sangye from 1097 to 1105, and the site of his famous meeting with Jetsun Milarepa.

two brothers give up *(mched po gnyis log pa):* Considering the context of the following song, I have understood this as a reference to two monks renouncing their vows. The phrase could also be translated as "two brothers returning."

8

at Langkor: According to Shes rab mgon, *Chos,* 3a, this event took place while Godrakpa was staying at Gyamring *(Rgyaṃ ring),* which is in the Langkor area. The disease Godrakpa contracted was probably leprosy, which he specifically mentions in song 2.

the propitiation: Godrakpa was practicing the propitiation of the deity Acala *(Mi g.yo ba),* who is a wrathful manifestation of Mañjuśrī. See Shes rab mgon, *Chos,* 3a.

the teachings on the Perfections: This would usually indicate the teachings of the Six Perfections, or the Sūtras on the Perfection of Transcendent Knowledge, but according to Shes rab mgon, *Chos,* 3a, Godrakpa was contemplating a text on the Four Truths in the tradition of the Pacification lineage *(zhi byed bden bzhi'i dpe gcig la gzigs rtog mdzad).*

in ten years: Shes rab mgon, *Chos,* 3a, says twelve years.

9

Gepa Sergyi Chagyib *(Gad pa Gser gyi bya skyibs):* This cave complex near Mt. Tise was an ancient Zhang Zhung holy place until the late ninth century, when it came under Buddhist control. During Godrakpa's lifetime the meditation site was held by followers of the Drukpa Kagyu *('Brug pa Bka' brgyud)* tradition up until the year 1215, after which it belonged to the Drigung Kagyu *('Bri gung Bka' brgyud).* In later centuries many of the caves collapsed into the lake. Now there are a few small meditation caves inhabited by Drigung Kagyu monks. See Vitali (1996), 399, note 651; 409, etc.

As a result of his intense meditation practice at Lake Mapham *(Mtsho Ma pham),* Godrakpa is said to have beheld the true state of the vajra body *(rdo rje lus kyi gnas lugs),* seen many exterior pure lands, and had a vision of the goddess Vajravārāhī. See Shes rab mgon, *Chos,* 4b.

demonic impediment *(gdon 'gegs):* According to the late Dezhung Rinpoche, there are two forces at work here. The term *gdon* refers to demonic beings that cause harm if offended, but not otherwise. *'Gegs* are nastier by nature, and cause harmful impediments all the time.

marks and characteristics *(mtshan dang dpe byad):* These refer to the thirty-two major physical marks and eighty minor characteristics of a buddha.

10

the obscurations of the afflicting emotions will surely be incinerated. ...keep intrinsic awareness clear!: These lines are not a direct translation, since several syllables are illegible in the original Tibetan text. Although an accurate translation is impossible, I have filled in the blanks with a few hypothetical phrases to make the song read smoothly.

11

Tashi Khangmar *(Bkra shis khang dmar):* According to Shes rab mgon, *Chos,* 5a, Godrakpa spent time teaching at this monastery at the invitation of the master Uyukpa, and there gained realization of the truthless nature of appearances. Uyukpa Rikpey Senge (*'U yug pa Rigs pa'i seng ge,* d. 1253) was the foremost disciple of Sakya Paṇḍita in the field of epistemology *(pramāṇa, tshad ma).*

three delights *(mnyes pa gsum):* The three ways to delight a master are by practicing meditation, which is the best; by service with body and speech, which is middling; and by material offerings, which is inferior.

departed into space *(dgung du gshegs):* a euphemism for death.

removal of impediments *(gags sel):* This refers to techniques used for the removal of impediments encountered in meditation practice. As mentioned in the introduction, such techniques were Godrakpa's special field of expertise.

final two sets of mantra *(sngags phyi ma gnyis):* an obscure phrase. Perhaps it is a reference to the yoga tantras and the highest yoga tantras.

12

three officials and four friends *(drung gsum dang gnyen gzhi):* unidentified.

fivefold degeneracy *(snyings ma lnga):* These five are degeneracy of lifespan, view, afflicting emotions, sentient beings, and the times.

13

Kagyu *(Bka' brgyud):* There are many different Kagyu traditions in Tibet. The most famous lineages are based on the teachings of Indian adepts such as Saraha, Nāropa, and Maitripa, and were brought to Tibet primarily by Marpa Lotsawa in the eleventh century.

honored on everyone's heads: In tantric meditation the teachers in a lineage are sometimes visualized above one's head.

two goals *(don gnyis):* benefit for oneself and benefit for others.

brings phenomena to the point of cessation *(chos rnams zad sar skyol ba):* This is primarily an expression from the Great Seal tradition. Godrakpa's main disciple, Gyalwa Yangönpa, explains it at length in one of his songs. Briefly, it indicates the place where all the phenomena of saṃsāra and nirvāṇa eventually go. This is an unfabricated state of mind, unimpeded radiant emptiness, like the clear sky, which is synonymous with the enlightened awareness of the buddhas, and is the true characteristic of the minds of all sentient beings. See Yang dgon pa, *Dpal,* 468–71. A similar expression is also found in the Nyingma tradition.

three buddha bodies: See note to song 5.

E Ma: an exclamation of wonder.

14

Semikpa *(Se mig pa):* As mentioned above, Godrakpa received novice lay vows and many teachings, such as the Path with the Result, from this master.

15

the assemblies: The two assemblies of merit and primordial awareness must be completed for the attainment of enlightenment.

the buddha body of form *(gzugs sku):* The buddha body of form is composed of the emanation buddha body and the buddha body of rapture.

16

cherished object *(rme zan):* Tulku Sangak Rinpoche suggested the spelling *smar zan,* an archaic term for a most precious thing, whether food or other possessions.

a human body is like a pea stuck to a wall: a traditional example used to illustrate the rare and unique nature of human life. If a handful of peas is thrown against a wall, what are the odds that even one pea will stick to the wall rather than fall to the ground? The odds of being born as a human being are said to be much less than that.

the six realms: According to traditional Buddhism, the six realms of existence are those of hell beings, hungry ghosts, animals, human beings, demi-gods, and gods.

absorption and maintenance *(mnyam rjes):* The term "absorption" *(mnyam bzhag)* refers to meditation during a formal session, and "maintenance" *(rjes thob)* refers to sustaining the meditative state of mind at other times.

bring phenomena to the point of cessation: See note to song 13.

sacred commitments *(dam tshig):* In general, there are fourteen basic and eight branch sacred commitments involved in the practice of the Vajrayāna.

18

spiritual warmths and signs *(drod rtags):* Briefly, the term "spiritual warmth" refers to earlier experiences that herald the arising of later "signs," like the appearance of smoke before fire. It is a mistake to regard these spiritual warmths and signs to be results in themselves.

19

Zegyi Gekung *(Zad kyi rgad khung):* In Shes rab mgon, *Chos*, 4b, the spelling is Zar gyi rgod khungs. The monastery and temple of Gökung *(Rgod khung)* is an ancient site in the western kingdom of Burang *(Pu hrang)*. See Vitali (1996), 404, notes 661–62, etc.

the Great Brahmin: the Indian adept Saraha, author of *The Dohā Trilogy* and a main source for the teachings of the Great Seal.

a flash *(sog srun):* an obscure term; translation uncertain.

20

a beautiful woman: According to Shes rab mgon, *Chos*, 4a, this woman was the Indian adept Lady Lakṣmīṅkarā, and the event occurred just before Godrakpa took full monastic ordination at the age of twenty-eight. The lines of verse are also recorded in the biography, but with very different spellings.

the three piṭakas *(sde snod gsum):* the three collections of the basic teachings of Buddhism in the Sūtras, the Abhidharma, and the Vinaya.

creation and perfection *(skyed rdzogs):* All the practices of tantric Buddhism are included in the two categories of creation stage *(bskyed rim)* and perfection stage *(rdzogs rim)* meditation.

21
Verses almost identical to the opening lines of this song are also found in a song of the early Kagyu master Lingchen Repa (*Gling chen ras pa,* 1128–88). See Gling chen ras pa, *Rje,* 138: *'chi ba sems kyi me long yin/ 'chi rgyu 'dug gam mi 'dug ltos/ ji srid 'chi bas 'jigs kyi bar/ da dung rtogs pa'i nyams myong spel//.* The next verses in Lingchen Repa's song are also very similar to the following ones in Godrakpa's song.

Māra *(Bdud):* see note to song 2.

22
Siddhi Phalam *(si ti pha la ma):* Sanskrit for "the result *(phalam)* of spiritual attainment *(siddhi).*" A similar expression is found at the end of song 2.

like an inquisitive girl, a teacher may be able to inquire closely about others but, if inquired about in return, may eventually become embarrassed: The translation of these lines is very uncertain. Tulku Sangak Rinpoche felt that the text was seriously corrupt, and could not make sense of the passage.

23
the three lower realms: the realms of the hell beings, hungry ghosts, and animals.

24
six grains *('bru drug):* A traditional list of the five grains includes barley, rice, wheat, pea, and sesame. A different list adds buckwheat, which is perhaps the sixth included here.

nectar *(sris):* Tulku Sangak Rinpoche suggested a spelling of *srus,* which is a term for freshly mashed ears of grain. These are considered a great delicacy and are used to make a delicious soup.

25
Oṃ Maṇi Padme Hūṃ: the mantra of Avalokiteśvara, the divine embodiment of compassion for all sentient beings.

External apprehended objects like hidden treasure: At first one does not realize that phenomena apprehended by the mind as externally existing are a delusion.

Internal apprehending mind like discovered treasure: Then one realizes that what appear to be external phenomena are actually without self-nature, and are only appearances of the apprehending mind itself.

26

According to Tulku Sangak Rinpoche's interpretation of this song, the **meltwater** *(rul chu)* that floods from the melting of a glacier must be quickly channeled or carried to the fields for irrigation before it flows away. By the time the white **daisies** *(rtsi thog)* **spread on the valley floor** *(rlungs* should be read as *klung),* the livestock have already wandered off into the mountains, and it is too late to tend them. At the end of the season the crops ripen and the meadows are **yellow** and must be harvested on time.

clay slopes of Rumbu *(logs rum bu'i rdza):* This may be a reference to a western area in Guge *(Gu ge),* which is known as Rumbu. See Vitali (1996), 252–54, etc.

four examples and five points: The four examples are in the first sentence of each verse. The first four points are made in the last sentence of each verse. Death, when everything is gone, is the fifth point.

27

marsh *(na ma):* The original Tibetan was missing a syllable and read only *na'i,* which has been corrected in the Tibetan text to the complete form of *na ma'i* at the suggestion of Tulku Sangak Rinpoche.

young yaks and lambs *(be lug):* an obscure term explained by Tulku Sangak Rinpoche.

cutting and threshing *(rtsas g.yul):* an obscure term explained by Tulku Sangak Rinpoche as the cutting and threshing of grain during the autumn harvest.

28

at Langkor: Shes rab mgon, *Chos,* 6a, specifies that this retreat was in the White Residence *(Gzims dkyil dkar po),* which is at Langkor, and says that there were four ḍākinīs. The White Residence is perhaps another name for the shrine where the remains of Phadampa Sangye were kept. See note to song 37.

the eight charnel grounds: These charnel grounds, or cemeteries, were originally located in the Indian subcontinent and play a role in the spiritual topography of the highest yoga tantras. According to Dudjom (1991), vol. 2, 157, the eight charnel grounds are named the Most Fierce *(gtum drag),* Dense Thicket *(tshang tshing 'khrigs pa),* Dense Blaze *('bar 'khrigs pa),* Endowed with Skeletons *(keng rus can),*

Cool Forest *(bsil bu tshal,* Skt. *Śītavana),* Black Darkness *(mun pa nag po),* Resonant with "Kilikili" *(ki li ki lir sgra sgrog pa),* and Wild Laughter of "Ha ha" *(ha ha rgod pa).*

Jambu continent *('Dzam gling):* In Buddhist cosmology according to the Abhidharma, this world system is composed of four major continents surrounding the cosmic Mt. Meru. Human beings inhabit the southern Jambu continent, or Jambudvīpa. The same term is also commonly used for the Indian subcontinent.

Uḍḍiyana *(U rgyan):* Usually identified with the Swat Valley region of modern Pakistan, Uḍḍiyana is regarded as a major source of tantric teachings and as the home of the ḍākinīs.

29

Rāhu *(Gza'):* Traditionally it is thought that eclipses occur when the sun or moon is seized and swallowed by the monster Rāhu.

30

floods *(grub):* The spelling should be corrected to the homophone *brub.*

six grains: See note to song 24.

31

intermediate state of existence *(srid pa bar do):* the intermediate state between death and rebirth.

plantain trees *(chu shing):* This tree, which is hollow on the inside, is often used as an example to illustrate that worldly phenomena have no essence.

hoarded *(so song):* Tulku Sangak Rinpoche suggested a spelling of *gsog srung,* which is a near homophone.

Upper Nyang *(Nyang stod):* Nyang is one of the main cultural areas of Tsang *(Gtsang)* Province in west central Tibet. The important center of Gyantse *(Rgyal rtse)* is located in the Upper Nyang Valley, as is the monastery of Zhalu *(Zhwa lu).*

the blessed site of Godrak: Godrakpa spent many years meditating in the cave of Godrak *(Ko brag),* or "Go Cliffs," and thus became known as the Dharma Lord Godrakpa. Important information about the location of Godrakpa's cave is found in Tāranātha, *Myang,* 116, 121, 123, and 148.

32

the Lord of Great Compassion at Gyirong: The Lord of Great Compassion *(Jo bo Thugs rje chen po)* is the famous Noble Wati *('Phag pa Wa ti)* image of Avalokiteśvara in the town of Gyirong *(Skyid grong)* near the Tibetan border with Nepal. This was one of the holiest images in Tibet. It was removed during the Chinese takeover of Tibet and is now housed in the private shrine of H.H. the Dalai Lama in Dharamsala, India. Shes rab mgon, *Chos*, 7b, mentions a visit to Gyirong by Godrakpa near the end of his life. During his stay Godrakpa made great offerings to the Avalokiteśvara image and distributed a huge amount of valuables, food, and so forth to the people of the area.

The food is eaten in nonduality, the taste experienced as great bliss: With the exception of the single word "food" *(zas)* in place of "flesh" *(sha)* in the original, these two lines are from a song by the Indian adept Śavaripa, who was also the source of the special direct transmission of the Six-Branch Yoga of Kālacakra, which Godrakpa received at Tingri Langkor from the Indian master Vibhūticandra. Śavaripa's original song is found in a collection of the songs of the eighty-four great adepts of India, which was compiled by the Indian master Vīraprabhāsvara *(Dpa' bo 'od gsal)*. See Dpa' bo 'od gsal, *Grub*, 139.5. The same lines, exactly as found in Śavaripa's song, are also repeated in song 43. See the note to song 43 for a translation of Śavaripa's song. See Stearns (1996), 139, n. 46, for a brief biographical sketch of Śavaripa in the tradition of Vibhūticandra.

Lama Khandro *(Bla ma Mkha' 'gro):* Perhaps Godrakpa's companion on this occasion was Lhasu Lungpa Khandro *(Lha sru lung pa Mkha' 'gro)*, one of the disciples through whom his tradition of the Path with the Result was passed down. See Ngor chen Kun dga' bzang po, *Lam*, 116.2.

34

According to Shes rab mgon, *Chos*, 3a, when Godrakpa was staying in a small guesthouse on Mt. Shrī *(Shrī ri)* he saw others sleeping outside in the snow and rain. Out of compassion, he then built two large guesthouses modeled on a fine house of the area.

The translations **residence** *(gdung khang)* and **house of the body** *(zug khang)* follow the spelling corrections *gzhugs khang* and *gzugs khang* suggested by Tulku Sangak Rinpoche. The human body is often metaphorically referred to as a container or house in the songs of Jetsun Milarepa.

35

King Tobgyel *(Mnga' bdag Stobs rgyal):* This king can be identified as Tobgyel Dey *(Stobs rgyal lde)* of the Burang *(Pu hrangs)* royal line, who was active in the first or second quarter of the thirteenth century. See Vitali (1996), 383, n. 615, and 432, n. 719. Shes rab mgon, *Chos*, 9a, also mentions that Godrakpa was honored by a king referred to by the same title of *Mnga' bdag*.

Sandalwood in the land of Malaya *(Ma la'i yul):* This may refer to Mt. Mālaya in southern India, which was covered with sandal trees. See Krang dbyi sun, ed., *Bod*, vol. 2, 2678, for a description.

six fine herbs *(bzang po drug):* These six herbs are beneficial to specific organs in the body: nutmeg *(dzā ti)* for the heart, aragonite *(cu gang)* for the lungs, saffron *(gur gum)* for the liver, clove *(li shi)* for the spinal cord *(srog rtsa?)*, cardamom *(sug smel)* for the kidneys, and cubeb *(ka ko la)* for the spleen. See Krang dbyi sun, ed., *Bod*, vol. 2, 2512.

land of Cāmara *(Rnga yab yul):* This may refer to either the land of Uḍḍiyana *(U rgyan)* or to one of the eight minor subcontinents, which is located to the west of the Jambu continent in traditional Buddhist cosmology.

you'll speak in praise of me later: As mentioned in the preface to this song, the people of Tsayo were disgruntled with Godrakpa for some unspecified reason. Here he points out that they may not appreciate him at the moment, but when he dies, they'll all be singing his praises and saying what a great master he was.

36

Trakar *(Brag mkhar):* This may be a corrupt and abbreviated form of Tragar Daso *(Brag dkar rta so)*, a famous site where Jetsun Milarepa meditated. Tulku Sangak Rinpoche suggested the spelling of *dbar* instead of the *dbyar* found at the end of the editor's concluding sentance.

37

the White Mausoleum *(Sku gdung dkar):* the shrine where the remains of the Indian master Phadampa Sangye were kept at Tingri Langkor. At the end of the sixteenth century the Jonang master Tāranātha visited the White Mausoleum and saw an image of Phadampa with a vermilion face, as well as a special image of Godrakpa that was also kept there. See Tāranātha, *Rgyal*, 178.

the Mahābodhi *(Byang chub chen po):* This is the great shrine marking the place where Buddha Śākyamuni attained full enlightenment at Bodhgayā in India. The equal sanctity of the White Mausoleum and the Mahābodhi shrine was a traditional comparison in Tingri. See Aziz (1979), 37.

I saw the circumambulation path blocked...: According to Tulku Sangak Rinpoche, in this song Godrakpa is probably reporting several sights he beheld in a vision. The obstacle to the circumambulation path was perhaps cleared away when he prayed to the Three Jewels, and so forth, invoking the truth of their blessings.

38

Several lines in this song are clearly inspired by an earlier song of Jetsun Milarepa. See Rus pa'i rgyan can (= Gtsang smyon He ru ka), *Rnal,* 436–37, and Chang (1962), vol. 1, 280–81. My thanks go to Hubert Decleer for pointing this out.

Zhangdön, Ngogchung, and Nyelgom: The master Zhangdön Semikpa *(Zhang ston Se mig pa)* was the teacher from whom Godrakpa first received the novice vows of a Buddhist layman when he was eighteen years old, and a number of important initiations and teachings, such as the Path with the Result. Curiously, the master referred to here as Ngogchung *(Sngog chung)* isn't mentioned anywhere else. Perhaps this name is used to refer to another teacher who was better known by a different name. The master Nyelgom *(Snyel sgom)* was another early teacher. Also see the notes to song 1.

Hayagrīva with Vārāhī, Pacification, and the Path with the Result: Hayagrīva with Vārāhī *(Brta' Phag)* refers to the deity Hayagrīva *(Rta mgrin)* and his consort Vajravārāhī *(Rdo rje phag mo).* The practices of these two deities together is very common, especially in the Nyingma tradition. The Pacification *(Zhi byed)* teachings were brought to Tibet by the Indian master Phadampa Sangye in the eleventh century, and although once widespread, are no longer a vital tradition. The teachings of the Path with the Result *(Lam 'bras)* have been discussed in the introduction, and are now maintained as the most significant system of tantric meditation in the Sakya tradition.

mountain grass *(rngad):* definition provided by Tulku Sangak Rinpoche.

40

a dragon year *(brug lo):* probably the dragon year of 1244. See the following note.

a fine Vijayā temple *(rnam par rgyal ma'i khang zangs):* Probably a reference to the construction of a *vijayāstūpa (rnam rgyal mchod rten),* which is one of the eight traditional types of stūpas. According to Shes rab mgon, *Chos,* 6b, Godrakpa built a stūpa *('bum pa)* for the benefit of his late mother at Langkor soon after the repulsion of a Mongolian army *(hor dmag zlog pa),* and also constructed a large residence *(gzims khang chen mo)* during the same period. The Indian master Vibhūticandra's letter to Godrakpa also arrived at Langkor during this time. Taking into account the chronology of both Vibhūticandra's and Godrakpa's lives, the most probable date for this song is 1244.

41

That spacious site of Tingri: There is a possible play on words here. The term *yangs pa can,* here translated as "spacious," is also the Tibetan translation of the Sanskrit name Vaiśāli, which was an important retreat site for Śākyamuni Buddha, as Tingri Langkor was for Phadampa Sangye, the founder of the Pacification tradition in Tibet.

Indian Lord: Phadampa Sangye, who founded the hermitage at Tingri Langkor.

the evil Mongols: Shes rab mgon, *Chos,* 6b, mentions the repelling of a Mongol army *(hor dmag zlog pa).* As discussed in the notes to the translation of song 40, this event can tentatively be dated to shortly before the dragon year of 1244. In Roerich (1976), 679, it is mentioned that Godrakpa made a request for twenty-three teachers to perform a rite for averting the danger of a Mongol attack. The term *hor nag po* is translated here as "evil Mongols." According to Vitali (1996), 287, the term *hor nag mo* is a literal translation of the name Qarakhanid, the Turkic tribe ruling Southern Turkistan from the tenth century. But this may be too early to apply here, since the Qarakhanids lost their kingdom in the twelfth century. Perhaps the name continued to be used in Tibetan for other aggressors, such as the Mongols?

42

Gangā: the famous Indian river Ganges, whose headwaters are traced to Lake Mapham in west Tibet.

Ü and Tsang *(Dbus gtsang):* the two provinces of Central Tibet.

43

Dradum in Tsang *(Tsam Pra dum):* see note 49 in the introduction. The appearance of two women and the image of hunting on a mountain are definite allusions to the story of the Indian adept Śavaripa. He was a hunter, and is always depicted carrying a bow and arrows, and accompanied by his two consorts as they hunt wild beasts on the mountain of Śrīparvata.

Chagi Gyagya *(Chag gi skya skya):* According to Mang thos Klu sgrub rgya mtsho, *Bstan,* 222, Chag Gyagya *(Chag skyar skya)* is the name of a place in Tsang.

The flesh is eaten in nonduality, the taste experienced as great bliss: These lines are from a song by Śavaripa, and are also found in song 32. Śavaripa's original song is found in a collection of the songs of the eighty-four great adepts of India, which was compiled by the Indian master Vīraprabhāsvara *(Dpa' bo 'od gsal).* See Dpa' bo 'od gsal, *Grub,* 139.5. Because of the striking similarities between the songs of Śavaripa and Godrakpa, a translation of the original song is given here:

Guru Śavaripa said,

In the forest grove of ignorance
the wild beasts of subject and object circulate.
Drawing the bow of both skillful means
and transcendent knowledge, I fire the arrow
of the essential meaning.
Thoughts are what die.
The flesh is eaten in nonduality,
the taste experienced as great bliss.
The result of the Great Seal is achieved.

44
Verses quite similar to the final two quatrains of this song are also found in song 5.

Colophon
E Ma Ho: an exclamation of wonder.

three worlds *(srid gsum):* the same as the desire realm, form realm, and formless realm.

Rin Nam *(Rin rnams):* Lhatsun Rinchen Namgyel *(Lha btsun Rin chen rnam rgyal),* the original publisher of the Tibetan text.

Evaṃ: "Thus." A Sanskrit term used here to mark the end of the collection. The term also expresses the total integration of the transcendent knowledge of emptiness *(e),* and the skillful means of great bliss *(vaṃ).*

A final note in the text mentions that the wooden blocks for printing were cut by a certain Gendun *(Dge mdun).*

Bibliography

Tibetan Sources

Anonymous. *Kha rag gnyos kyi gdung rabs khyad par 'phags pa.* In *Kha-rag-gnyos kyi gdung-rabs and Rlangs-kyi po-ti bse-ru bsdus-pa.* Dolanji: Khedup Gyatso, 1978.

Kun dga' grol mchog, Jo nang. *Khrid brgya'i brgyud pa'i lo rgyus.* In *Gdams-ngag mdzod,* vol. 12, pp. 309–40. Delhi: N. Lungtok and N. Gyaltsan, 1972.

Ko brag pa Bsod nams rgyal mtshan. *Khams gsum 'dran bral grub thob ko rag pa'i mgur 'bum.* Nepal-German Manuscript Preservation Project, Microfilm Reel No. L 456/8. Xylograph, 16 fols. Folios 7 and 16 missing.

———. *Khams gsum 'dran bral grub thob ko rag pa'i mgur 'bum.* Collection of E. Gene Smith. Xylograph, 16 fols. Folio 6 missing.

———. *Lam 'bras snyan brgyud/ lam 'bras bu dang bcas pa' i gdams ngag.* In *Gzhung-bshad klog-skya-ma and Other Related Esoteric Sa-skya-pa Texts.* Tashi Dorje, Tibetan Bonpo Monastic Centre, 1975, vol. 1, pp. 405–590.

Krang dbyi sun, ed. *Bod rgya tshig mdzod chen mo.* 2 vols. Beijing: Mi rigs dpe skrun khang, 1993.

Gling chen Ras pa Padma rdo rje. *Rje grub thob chen po'i bka' 'bum las gsung mgur gyi rim pa.* In *The Collected Works (Bka'-'bum) of Gling-chen ras-pa Padma rdo-rje,* vol. 1. Tashijong: Khampa Gar Sungrab Nyamso Gyunphel Parkhang, 1985.

'Gos Lo tsā ba Gzhon nu dpal. *Deb ther sngon po.* 2 vols. Si khron mi rigs dpe skrun khang, 1984.

Ngag dbang blo bzang rgya mtsho, Tā la'i bla ma. *Zab pa dang rgya che ba'i dam pa'i chos kyi thob yig gangā'i chu rgyun.* Vol. 1. Delhi: Nechung and Lhakhar, 1970.

Ngor chen Kun dga' bzang po. *Lam 'bras bu dang bcas pa'i man ngag gi byung tshul gsung ngag rin po che bstan pa rgyas pa'i nyi 'od.* In *The Complete Works of the Great Masters of the Sa-skya Sect of Tibetan Buddhism (Sa-skya-pa'i bka'-'bum),* vol. 9, pp. 108–26. Tokyo: The Toyo Bunko, 1968.

'Jam mgon Kong sprul, Blo gros mtha' yas. *Theg pa'i sgo kun las btus pa gsung rab rin po che'i mdzod bslab pa gsum legs par ston pa'i bstan bcos shes bya kun khyab.* 3 vols. Beijing: Mi rigs dpe skrun khang, 1982.

'Jam mgon A mes zhabs Ngag dbang kun dga' bsod nams. *Yongs rdzogs bstan pa rin po che'i nyams len gyi man ngag gsung ngag rin po che'i byon tshul khog phub dang bcas pa rgyas par bshad pa legs bshad 'dus pa'i rgya mtsho.* In *The Tshogs-bshad Tradition of the Sa-skya Lam-'bras,* vol. 1, pp. 1–314. Dehra Dun: Sakya Centre, 1983.

'Jam dbyangs Mkhyen brtse dbang phyug. *Gdams ngag byung tshul gyi zin bris gsang chen bstan pa rgyas byed ces bya ba kha'u brag rdzong pa'i bzhed pa ma nor ba ban rgan mkhyen brtse'i nyams len.* In *The Slob-bshad Tradition of the Sa-skya Lam-'bras,* vol. 14, pp. 1–154. Dehra Dun: Sakya Centre, 1983.

Jñānavajra. *Gnyos rgyal ba lha nang pa'i rnam thar rin chen phreng ba yon tan gsal ba'i me long.* Vol. 2 of *Thon mi'i rig lam.* Dehra Dun: Drikung Kagyu Institute, 1997.

Tāranātha, Jo nang. *Rgyal khams pa tā ra nā thas bdag nyid kyi rnam thar nges par brjod pa'i deb ther/ shin tu zhib mo ma bcos lhug pa'i rtogs brjod.* Paro: Ngodrup and Sherab Drimay, 1978.

———. *Stag lung zhabs drung gi gsung lan.* In *The Collected Works of Jo-nang rje-btsun Tāranātha,* vol. 13, pp. 567–76. Leh: Smanrtsis Shesrig Dpemdzod, 1983.

———. *Rdo rje'i rnal 'byor gyi 'khrid yig mthong ba don ldan gyi lhan thabs 'od brgya 'bar.* In *The Collected Works of Jo-nang rje-btsun Tāranātha,* vol. 3, pp. 447–805. Leh: Smanrtsis Shesrig Dpemdzod, 1983.

———. *Myang yul stod smad bar gsum gyi ngo mtshar gtam gyi legs bshad mkhas pa'i 'jug ngogs.* Lhasa: Bod ljongs mi dmangs dpe skrun khang, 1983.

Bstan 'dzin Chos kyi blo gros, 'Bri gung. *Gsang lam sgrub pa'i gnas chen nyer bzhi'i ya gyal gau ḍā ri 'am 'brog la phyi gangs kyi ra ba'i sngon byung gi tshul las brtsams pa'i gtam gyi rab tu byed pa nyung ngu rnam gsal.* Gangtok: Sherab Gyaltsen, 1983.

Thu'u bkwan Blo bzang chos kyi nyi ma. *Thu'u bkwan grub mtha'.* Kansu: Mi rigs dpe skrun khang, 1984.

Padmasambhava. *Rgan mo mdzub btsug gi gdams ngag.* Title take from colophon. In *Gdams-ngag mdzod*, vol. 1, pp. 739–42. Delhi: N. Lungtok and N. Gyaltsan, 1972.

Padma gar dbang. *Zab chos sbas pa mig 'byed kyi chos bskor las paṇ che sha wa dbang phyug gi snyan rgyud rdo rje sum gyi bla ma rgyud pa'i rnam thar dad pa'i rnga chen.* Nepal-German Manuscript Preservation Project. Running No. L-4703. Reel No. L-450/6. Manuscript, 127 fols.

Dpa' bo 'od gsal (Vīraprabhāsvara). *Grub thob brgyad cu rtsa bzhi'i rtogs pa'i snying po (Caturaśīti siddha sambodhi hṛdaya).* In *The Tibetan Tripitaka: Peking Edition*, vol. 69, pp. 139.4.3–141.5.1. Tokyo-Kyoto: Tibetan Tripitaka Research Institute, 1957.

Mang thos Klu sgrub rgya mtsho. *Bstan rtsis gsal ba'i nyin byed lhag bsam rab dkar.* Lhasa: Bod ljongs mi dmangs dpe skrun khang, 1987.

Smon lam tshul khrims. *Mchims nam mkha' grags pa'i rnam thar.* Beijing: Library of the Cultural Palace of Minorities. Manuscript, 50 fols.

Tshar chen Blo gsal rgya mtsho. *Zab mo lus dkyil gyi rnam par bshad pa skal bzang snying gi padmo bzhad pa.* In *The Slob-bshad Tradition of the Sa-skya Lam-'bras*, vol. 10, pp. 514–79. Dehra Dun: Sakya Centre, 1983.

Tshe dbang nor bu, Kaḥ thog rig 'dzin. *Mar mi dwags po jo bo rje yab sras sogs dam pa 'ga' zhig gi rnam thar sa bon dus kyi nges pa brjod pa dag ldan nyung gsal.* In *Selected Writings of Kaḥ-thog rig-'dzin Tshe-dbang nor-bu*, vol. 1, pp. 669–705. Darjeeling: Kargyud Sungrab Nyamso Khang, 1973.

Yang dgon pa, Rgyal ba. *Rgyal ba yang dgon pa'i mgur 'bum.* In *Collected Works (Gsung-'bum) of Yang-dgon-pa Rgyal-mtshan-dpal*, vol. 3, pp. 165–376. Thimphu: Kunzang Topgey, 1976.

———. *Rdo rje lus kyi sbas bshad.* In *Collected Works (Gsung-'bum) of Yang-dgon-pa Rgyal-mtshan-dpal*, vol. 2, pp. 421–97. Thimphu: Kunzang Topgey, 1976.

———. *Dpal ldan yang dgon pa'i bka' 'bum yid bzhin nor bu'i phreng ba.* In *Collected Works (Gsung-'bum) of Yang-dgon-pa Rgyal-mtshan-dpal*, vol. 3, pp. 377–526. Thimphu: Kunzang Topgey, 1976.

Rin chen ldan, Spyan snga. *Rin po che lha gdong pa'i rnam thar bstod pa ma.* In *Collected Works (Gsung-'bum) of Yang-dgon-pa Rgyal-mtshan-dpal,* vol. 1, pp. 21–103. Thimphu: Kunzang Topgey, 1976.

Rus pa'i rgyan can (Gtsang smyon He ru ka). *Rnal 'byor gyi dbang phyug chen po mi la ras pa'i rnam mgur.* Kokonor: Mi rigs dpe skrun khang, 1989.

Shākya mchog ldan, Paṇ chen. *Smra sgo mtshon cha lta bu'i bstan bcos kyi rnam bshad smra ba'i rgyan.* In *The Complete Works* (*Gsung-'bum*) *of Gser-mdog Paṇ-chen Shākya mchog-ldan,* vol. 24, pp. 232–92. Thimphu: Kunzang Tobgey, 1975.

Shes rab mgon. *Chos rje ko brag pa'i rnam thar.* Beijing: Library of the Cultural Palace of Minorities. Manuscript, 10 fols.

———. *Ri chos brgyud tshul gyi lo rgyus.* In *Collected Works (Gsung-'bum) of Yang-dgon-pa Rgyal-mtshan-dpal,* vol. 1, pp. 1–9. Thimphu: Kunzang Topgey, 1976.

Sa chen Kun dga' snying po. *Lam 'bras gzhung bshad sras don ma.* In *The Slob-bshad Tradition of the Sa-skya Lam-'bras,* vol. 12, pp. 1–446. Dehra Dun: Sakya Centre, 1983.

———. *Gzhung rdo rje'i tshig rkang gi 'grel pa rnal 'byor gyi dbang phyug dpal sa skya pa chen po la khams pa sga theng gis zhus pa.* In *The Slob-bshad Tradition of the Sa-skya Lam-'bras,* vol. 29, pp. 149–491. Dehra Dun: Sakya Centre, 1983.

Secondary Sources

Aris, Michael (1979). *Bhutan: The Early History of a Himalayan Kingdom.* Warminster, U.K.: Aris & Phillips.

Aziz, Barbara Nimri (1979). "Indian Philosopher as Tibetan Folk Hero: Legend of Langkor: A New Source Material on Phadampa Sangye." *Central Asiatic Journal,* vol. XXIII, no. 1–2, pp. 19–37.

Chang, Garma C. C. (1962). *The Hundred Thousand Songs of Milarepa.* 2 vols. Seacaucus: University Books.

Davidson, Ronald (1981). "The *Litany of Names of Mañjuśrī:* Text and Translation of the *Mañjuśrīnāmasaṃgīti.*" In *Tantric and Taoist Studies in Honour of R. A. Stein,* ed. Michel Strickmann, vol. 1, pp. 1–69. Brussels: Institut Belge des Hautes Études Chinoises.

Dudjom Rinpoche, Jikdrel Yeshe Dorje (1991). *The Nyingma School of Tibetan Buddhism: Its Fundamentals and History.* Trans. Gyurme Dorje and Matthew Kapstein. Boston: Wisdom Publications.

Edou, Jérôme (1996). *Machig Labdrön and the Foundations of Chöd.* Ithaca, N.Y.: Snow Lion Publications.

Grönbold, Günter (1982). "Materialien zur Geschichte des Ṣaḍaṅga-yoga: III. Die Guru-Reihen im buddhistischen Ṣaḍaṅga-yoga." *Zentralasiatische Studien* 16: 337–47.

Guenther, Herbert (1993). *Ecstatic Spontaneity: Saraha's Three Cycles of Dohā.* Berkeley: Asian Humanities Press.

Huber, Toni (1997). "A Guide to the La-Phyi *Maṇḍala*: History, Landscape and Ritual in South-Western Tibet." In *Maṇḍala and Landscape.* Ed. A. W. Macdonald, pp. 233–86. New Delhi: D. K. Printworld (P.) Ltd.

Kapstein, Matthew (1996). "*gDams ngag*: Tibetan Technologies of the Self." In *Tibetan Literature: Studies in Genre.* Ed. José Cabezón and Roger Jackson, pp. 275–89. Ithaca, N.Y.: Snow Lion Publications.

van der Kuijp, Leonard W. J. (1994). "Apropos of Some Recently Recovered Texts Belonging to the *Lam 'bras* Teachings of the Sa-skya-pa and Ko-brag-pa."

Journal of the International Association of Buddhist Studies, vol. 17, no. 2, pp. 175–202.

Lhalungpa, Lobsang P., trans. (1977). *The Life of Milarepa.* New York: E. P. Dutton.

Roerich, George N., trans. (1976). *The Blue Annals.* Delhi: Motilal Banarsidass.

Smith, E. Gene (1969). "Preface" to *The Life of the Saint of Gtsaṅ.* Śata Piṭaka Series, vol. 79. New Delhi: International Acadamy of Indian Studies.

———. (1969b). "Introduction" to *Encyclopedia Tibetica: The Collected Works of Bo-dong Paṇ-chen Phyogs-las rnam-rgyal.* Vol. 4, pp. 1–7. Delhi: Tibet House.

———. (1970). "Introduction" to *Kongtrul's Encyclopedia of Indo-Tibetan Culture.* Śata Piṭaka Series, vol. 90. New Delhi: International Academy of Indian Culture.

Stearns, Cyrus (1996). "The Life and Tibetan Legacy of the Indian *Mahāpaṇḍita* Vibhūticandra." *Journal of the International Association of Buddhist Studies* vol. 19, no. 1, pp. 127–71.

———. *Luminous Lives: The Story of the Early Masters of the "Path with the Result" in Tibet.* (forthcoming)

Vitali, Roberto (1996). *The Kingdoms of Gu.ge Pu.hrang.* Dharamsala: Tho ling gtsug lag khang lo gcig stong 'khor ba'i rjes dran mdzad sgo'i go sgrig tshogs chung.

Index

ABOUT WISDOM

Wisdom Publications, a not-for-profit publisher, is dedicated to making available authentic Buddhist works by the world's leading Buddhist scholars. We publish our titles with the appreciation of Buddhism as a living philosophy and with the special commitment to preserve and transmit important works from all the major Buddhist traditions.

If you would like more information or a copy of our mail-order catalog, please contact us at:

Wisdom Publications
199 Elm Street
Somerville, Massachusetts 02144 USA
Telephone: (617) 776-7416 • Fax: (617) 776-7841
Email: info@wisdompubs.org • www.wisdompubs.org

THE WISDOM TRUST

As a not-for-profit publisher, Wisdom Publications is dedicated to the publication of fine Dharma books for the benefit of all sentient beings and dependent upon the kindness and generosity of sponsors in order to do so. If you would like to make a donation to Wisdom, please do so through our Somerville office. If you would like to sponsor the publication of a book, please write or e-mail us for more information.

Thank you.

Wisdom Publications is a non-profit, charitable 501(c)(3) organization and a part of the Foundation for the Preservation of the Mahayana Tradition (FPMT).